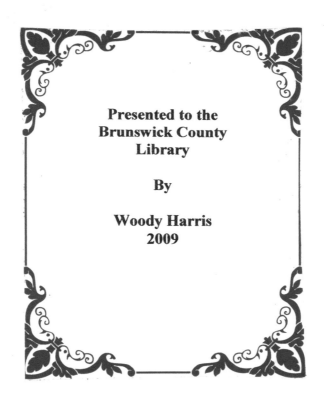

**Presented to the
Brunswick County
Library**

By

**Woody Harris
2009**

D1502634

Game of My Life
ATLANTA BRAVES

Jack Wilkinson

SportsPublishingLLC.com

ISBN 10: 1-59670-099-8
ISBN 13: 978-1-59670-099-4

© 2007 by Jack Wilkinson

Publishers: Peter L. Bannon and Joseph J. Bannon Sr.
Senior managing editor: Susan M. Moyer
Acquisitions editor: John Humenik
Developmental editor: Doug Hoepker
Art director: K. Jeffrey Higgerson
Dust jacket design: Dustin J. Hubbart
Interior layout: Kathryn R. Holleman
Photo editor: Erin Linden-Levy

Sports Publishing L.L.C.
804 North Neil Street
Champaign, IL 61820
Phone: 1-877-424-2665
Fax: 217-363-2073
SportsPublishingLLC.com

Printed in the United States of America

CIP data available upon request.

. . . AND LADIES OF THE CLUB:
JANET, KATHARINE, & ALI,
WITH LOVE AND AFFECTION.

CONTENTS

Chapter 1

DAVID JUSTICE

With one of the sweetest swings baseball had seen in years, David Justice changed everything: the Atlanta Braves' burgeoning reputation as the Buffalo Bills of baseball; the angry, even livid fan reaction to Justice's outspoken—if somewhat misconstrued—I-dare-you, incendiary words; the landscape of professional sports in Atlanta; and the enduring legacy of David Justice himself.

"That would have to be Game 6 of the World Series," Justice said, selecting the game of his life. "That would be No. 1."

The one and only world championship for the Atlanta Braves—baseball's dominant team in the first half of the '90s—was captured on the cool, crisp Atlanta evening of October 28, 1995. The night David Justice swung sweetly, and for posterity. Justice's solo home run into the right-field stands gave the Braves a 1-0 lead over the Cleveland Indians in the sixth inning. That lone run stood up, too, behind Tom Glavine's pitching, for the club's first World Series triumph since 1957.

With that, the Braves became the first franchise to win the world championship while based in three different cities: Boston,

Milwaukee, and Atlanta. With that, Justice—as talented as he was talkative, opinionated, and sometimes controversial—guaranteed himself a warm spot in Atlanta's heart and soul.

"But," he said in reflection, "there's so many other games to think of."

Let's re-think all this.

＊ ＊ ＊

If his two brief stints in Atlanta in 1989 officially constituted a thimble-sized cup of proverbial coffee, then David Justice formally and fully introduced himself in 1990: a 6-foot-3 shot of caffeinated talent and walk-the-walk style that made all of Atlanta—and soon all of baseball—stand up and take notice. How could you not? Smart and sassy and often sensational at the plate and sometimes afield, Justice was clearly a star-in-waiting. After graduating from high school in Cincinnati at the age of 16—he'd skipped the seventh and eighth grades—Justice played three years at Thomas More College in Kentucky and was drafted by Atlanta in 1985. He was only 19.

After working his way up through the organization—and absorbing the invaluable teachings and lessons afforded along the way—Justice arrived in Atlanta for good in 1990 as the Braves' new first baseman. At least when the season began. But when legend-in-residence Dale Murphy was traded to Philadelphia on August 4 of that year, life changed for David Justice—for good, and for the better.

"It was a combination of things that year," he said. "A change of position: they put me back in my natural position." In right field, where the vacancy caused by Murphy's departure fit Justice like an old worn shoe. "And it was also Clarence Jones, too," Justice said of the then-Braves hitting coach. "C.J. came to me and said, 'I want you to try this. David, if you try this, I guarantee your home runs will go up, your average will go up, and you'll be back in the running for the Rookie of the Year.'

"I said, 'You know what? I'll take my chances,'" Justice remembered. "I trusted him. He said, 'I want you to get real close to the plate—I was a natural pull hitter—and I want you to pull

everything. And I want you to hit nothing but fastballs. Only after they've gotten some strikes on you, then you swing.'

The trick worked: Justice crowded the plate, opposing pitchers began pounding him inside, and Justice began to hit—no, smote—all those fastballs. Justice finally gave up smoting for good at season's end. By then, his earlier struggles—he was batting .243 through 68 games, with eight homers and 28 RBIs—were but a distant memory. Switched back to right field, and armed with Jones' hitting insights, Justice relaxed and finished the season as the National League's hottest hitter. He led the league with 20 homers in the last two months (11 in August, plus nine more in September). His 28 homers and 78 runs batted in led all big-league rookies and tied Tigers' oversized slugger Cecil Fielder for the most home runs (23) after the All-Star break. "I got every first-place vote except one," said Justice, who easily won the NL Rookie of the Year voting. Montreal's Delino DeShields got that wayward first-place vote as Justice became the first Brave since Bob Horner in '78 to win the award.

For Justice and all his mates, 1991 changed everything. Justice was leading the league with 51 RBIs when he hurt his back and had to go on the disabled list for nearly two months in late June. "It was weird," Justice said. "I remember we were in Montreal and my back was sore. I played that night. Next night? I was so sore, I couldn't play. The day I couldn't play, Otis Nixon set a record with six stolen bases.

"I actually had a stress fracture in my back," he said. "But it didn't show up on an X-ray and didn't show up 'til next spring training."

By then, Justice and the Braves had begun their run to greatness down the '91 stretch in pursuit of Los Angeles. "I raked when I came back," he recalled. "When I came back, we just took off. That was the year I hit the home run off Dibble in the ninth."

Upon Justice's return on August 21, Atlanta closed 31-14 (a .688 winning percentage) with him back in the lineup and in right field. The Dibble game occurred in Cincinnati on October 1, a day in which Justice became the hometown hero in his old hometown of Cincinnati. With five games left, Atlanta was a game behind L.A. in the NL West standings. With just three innings gone that night in Cincinnati, the Braves were down 3-0 to Jose Rijo, the Reds' imposing, right-handed, No. 1 starter. By the ninth inning, however, Atlanta had closed to within a run at 6-5. Enter Dibble, Cincinnati's caveman closer, who walked Mark Lemke to lead off the bottom of the ninth.

"That was one of the best games. I remember that moment vividly," Justice said. "I remember Rob Dibble would always throw me first-pitch fastballs away. Terry Pendleton had just made an out. He came back by me when I was in the on-deck circle and said, 'Dave, pick me up.'

"I was trying to hit it up the middle, but I pulled it and it was a home run. That pitch was 101 mph. I knew it was gone. We went through Jose Rijo, Norm Charlton, Randy Myers, and Dibble to win that game."

Back home that weekend, everything changed forever for Justice and the Braves. "On Saturday, we came out against Houston," he said. "That's the one where I caught the ball, with my [arm raised in celebration]. I put it up before I even caught it." Once he caught the fly ball in right field for the final out, the Braves celebrated clinching at least a tie for the division title. But there was so much more before that.

"I remember all the tomahawks that season," Justice said. "And a packed house in Atlanta that day. That was unheard of in the past. We were a young team. People were saying we were going to fold. The Dodgers had all the veterans. [Darryl] Strawberry had said they weren't worried about us. But I thought, 'If we lose, it won't be because we're young. It'll be because we just lost. We were winning in the minor leagues. In 1989 [at Richmond], we won the Governor's Cup. I remember hugging Jim Beauchamp then; he was our manager. I said, 'Beach, we can do this in the big leagues.' And two years later, we were in the World Series."

Justice paused, took a breath, then resumed on a roll. "Here's one thing the Braves don't get credit for, and still do it—the way they develop players," he said. "Me, [Ron] Gant, [Jeff] Blauser, Lemke, [John] Smoltz, Glavine. The next generation was Chipper [Jones], Javy [Lopez], [Ryan] Klesko. The big three, all young. Then Andruw [Jones]. Then here comes [Rafael] Furcal, [Marcus] Giles, all young kids. The Braves are the best at developing young kids and getting 'em in the big leagues.

"Why? Our Single-A pitching coach in 1986 at Sumter was Leo Mazzone. *Leo Mazzone!*" Justice gushed. "Our hitting coach? Clarence Jones. . . . And we had [Hall of Famer] Willie Stargell floating around. We had quality coaches in the minor leagues. The Braves taught you how to play the game. When we came to the big leagues, we were ready."

That proper upbringing and tutelage was evident in Justice's performance in the 1991 World Series versus Minnesota. He homered off Scott Erickson in Game 3, then scored the winning run on Lemke's two-out single in the bottom of the 11th of that 5-4 triumph. Justice homered again in the 14-5 Game 5 cakewalk, his five RBIs tying the record for runs batted in by a National League player in a World Series game. In Game 6, Justice recalled, "I had Scott Erickson set up for another home run. I pulled it just foul." Kirby Puckett didn't, though; his 11th-inning homer off Charlie Leibrandt forced a Game 7.

"I remember the Lonnie Smith thing vividly," Justice said. "I remember him on first, and when Terry hit it, we just started screaming. That's an automatic double and an automatic run." Not exactly. In the eighth inning of that scoreless, dramatic, climactic Game 7, even when Smith hesitated on Pendleton's double to left-center and only advanced to third base, "I thought, 'Okay, it's second and third, Ronnie [Gant] is up. We're okay," Justice said. "Ronnie swings at the first pitch, hits a little dribbler to first. Kent Hrbek fields it, looks the runners back, and steps on the bag.

"They walk me, then [Sid] Bream hits into a 3-2-3 double play," he said. "I've only thrown a helmet maybe twice in my career. That night was the first time. I threw it down at second."

Two innings later, the Twins prevailed 1-0 to win the World Series. "That World Series hurt," Justice said. "It really hurt. I didn't know if we were going to be back in the World Series. The next year, Toronto was really good. I can live with that."

To have the chance to return to the '92 World Series against Toronto, the Braves first had to defeat the Pirates. In the bottom of the ninth inning, with the Braves trailing Pittsburgh 2-1 and two out,

Justice was on third base when pinch hitter Francisco Cabrera came to bat against Pittsburgh reliever Stan Belinda. "That moment in time, I still remember exactly what I was thinking," Justice said. "When Cabrera had two balls and one strike, I was thinking, 'He's going to hit a home run right here.' He was one of the best fastball hitters ever.

"I remember it being sold out and very loud," he said. "So loud that Jimy Williams [Atlanta's third-base coach] had to walk up and almost kiss my ear to tell me what he was saying. He wasn't really saying anything. Just pretending, where they might think a squeeze [play] was on."

The squeeze play wasn't on, and Cabrera didn't homer. After ripping a foul ball down the third-base line, Cabrera instead singled to left and into history. "I score," Justice said, "and I turn around, and I see Barry." Barry Bonds, the Pirates' left fielder who would win his first National League MVP award that year, was now in desperate pursuit of Cabrera's hit. "He's going toward left-center field, took a little angle," said Justice, who'd scored easily and was watching the play develop from behind home plate. "I'm thinking, 'Sid's got this easy.' I'm not even waving my arms [down]. All of a sudden, I see Sid coming and the ball coming, and Sid's got like a monkey on his back. I start jumping up and down, yelling, 'Get down! Get down!'"

Bream followed those frantic Justice instructions and scored fine, thank you. "I remember jumping on Sid, and I roll over and my feet are straight up in the air," he said. "Everybody's jumping up in the air and my feet are straight up in the air in the pile. But it was a great moment.

"Oh, my God, it was pandemonium," he said. "Unbelievable!"

Right then, amidst a pile-up of epic proportions, a memory flashed inside Justice's mind: The 1991 NLCS, Three Rivers Stadium in Pittsburgh, just before the start of Game 6. "Barry Bonds, Bobby Bonilla, and I are standing on the left-field line," Justice said. "We've got to win two games. Barry's telling me, 'Hey, man, you guys had a good run.' He's like, 'It's over.'"

Barry Bonds, wrong again. Fast forward to 1993. To the All-Star Game at Camden Yards in Baltimore's Inner Harbor. "Barry's with San Francisco," said Justice, a first-time NL All-Star that summer. "We're down nine games to the Giants at the break. He says to me, 'We got it.'" Barry Bonds, wrong yet again. Imagine that. The Braves' remarkable second-half run enabled them to edge the Giants by one scant game. The last great pennant race—before the strike ended the '94 season prematurely, and the wild card debuted in '95—concluded with Atlanta's heroic, but oh-so-draining, chase. "It killed us," Justice said of that fateful race. "And the Phillies were the only team that gave us trouble that year. It took so much out of us just to catch the Giants, we were spent."

Justice was magnificent in 1993. He belted 40 home runs, had 120 RBIs, and 24 steals. He won the first of his two Silver Sluggers, started in the All-Star Game, and finished third in the MVP voting. The 1995 season, of course, was decided by Justice's sweet swing. More, much more on that to follow. For now, consider 1996, and what might have been for Justice and the reigning world champion Braves.

"I was hurt," said Justice, who played just 40 games in '96 due to assorted injuries. "In August, I started taking batting practice. I was crushing the ball. Guys were, like, 'Dude, are you coming back?' When the playoffs started, they asked me if I could play. I thought, 'Maybe the World Series.'"

But Justice never played that postseason. He couldn't. Not that he was needed in the first round. Even with rookie Jermaine Dye struggling terribly at the plate while playing right field in Justice's stead, the Braves swept away the Dodgers 3-0 in the NL Division Series. After winning the opener of the NLCS against St. Louis, the Braves dropped three straight games and were on the cusp of extinction. By then, Justice felt healthy physically and ready to return to the lineup. "But they didn't ask me," he said. "That told me two things. One, that they felt they could win without me. And two, if I play and we win, and I do well, then how can they trade me the next year?"

Down 3-1 to the Cardinals, the Braves responded with an emphatic "BOOM!" They crushed Todd Stottlemyre 14-0 in Game 5, Javy Lopez and Mark Lemke and Fred McGriff fueling an LCS-record 22 hits that sent the series back to Atlanta. Greg Maddux was vintage Maddux in a 3-1 equalizer in Game 6. When Tom Glavine got a six-run cushion in the bottom of the first inning in Game 7, he coasted to a 15-0 rout. The Braves' new LCS record for runs in a game propelled them into their fourth World Series in five played.

Come the World Series, however, after the Braves surged to a 2-0 lead over the Yankees, outscoring them 16-1, and then led 6-0 after five innings of Game 4, Atlanta self-imploded. Jim Leyritz's pinch-hit, three-run homer of closer Mark Wohlers' woebegone splitter tied it in the eighth. New York won it in the 10th, then captured one-run affairs in Games 5 and 6 to launch the latest Yankee dynasty. Justice watched it all from the dugout. He wasn't on the roster. Dye was in right field the night of Game 5, and he crossed in front of center fielder Marquis Grissom on Cecil Fielder's fourth-inning drive in the right-center gap. The ball glanced off Grissom's glove—Dye having impeded his vision—and the night's only run scored.

"And I went to spring training the next year," Justice recalled, "and there were rumors that Freddie [McGriff] or I was going to be traded. Freddie's a great guy. He's not going to say anything. I asked [general manager John] Schuerholz, and he said, 'I'd bet my family and my home that you will not be traded.' You can't get a better confirmation than that. So I go into the clubhouse and say, 'Fellas, I'm still here!'"

Not for long. On the day the Braves were breaking camp in West Palm Beach, coach Ned Yost told Justice, "DJ, Bobby wants to see you." Bobby Cox was waiting in his office, along with Schuerholz. "I saw them," Justice said, "and I said, 'Okay, where am I going?'" Destination: Cleveland. Heading along with him was Grissom, in exchange for Kenny Lofton and Alan Embree.

"That tore my heart out," Justice recalled. "But they really tore out Marquis' heart. He was from Atlanta. Still lives south of Atlanta. I came out of Bobby's office, and guys are hugging me. After the third guy, I said, 'Guys, I can't take it. I'm gonna be crying.' And I left.

"All I ever wanted to be was a Brave," Justice said. "That's the team that brought me up. Every trade after that was pure business. But that one really hurt me. The Braves were family."

Cleveland, however, proved revelatory. "Life in Cleveland was *great*," said Justice. "I always tell people, 'It's like going from living with your family to living with your cousins.' I'm back in my home state, three hours from Cincinnati.

"And those fans?" he said. "We sold out every single night. Man, shoot, those fans were great. There's a team that deserves to win a championship. I hope the Tribe wins another World Series someday."

Cleveland should have won the Series in Justice's first season playing on the shores of Lake Erie. But closer Jose Mesa blew Game 7 and the upstart Florida Marlins won the first of their two World Series. Justice—who was spectacular that season, with an AL-leading .329 average, 33 homers, 101 RBIs, and a career-best .596 slugging percentage—was disappointed, but not crushed. "I thought, 'I've already won one World Series. I can't be greedy. God can't smile on me every day. He's gotta smile on the pitcher sometime,'" Justice said, laughing. "I'd already ripped the heart out of Jim Leyland twice with Pittsburgh [where Leyland was managing the Pirates in the '91 and '92 NLCS, before taking over the expansion Marlins]. He's a great man. And down in Florida, the Lord shined on him."

For Justice, who drew six walks and had four RBIs against Florida but batted just .185, the consolation was the road to the World Series. "My best year was '97. Easily," he said. "I only had two bad weeks. I felt like I got a hit every day. It was my best year as far as consistency. Just daily. Oh, man."

Justice and the Indians won AL Central Division titles again in 1998 and '99, but their World Series days were over. Justice would have to leave town once again to return to baseball's grandest stage. He did so, in baseball's grandest setting: Yankee Stadium, as a New York Yankee. He was traded in late June of 2000 to the Yanks for Ricky Ledee, Jake Westbrook, and Zach Day. In the Bronx, Justice continued his hot hitting. "In 2000, that was my best year from beginning to end," he said. "I had 21 homers with Cleveland; then I hit 20 with the Yankees." He finished with a career-high 41 and, once again, savored baseball's ultimate high: Another world championship.

"The one thing about the Yankees—it's a whole different thing coming out of that home dugout than the visitors dugout," he said. "The Yankees expect to win every day. They got history. They've got great fans. I came in hot; I was swinging well. And I just exploded. That was a great year."

The Yankees barely survived Oakland in the AL Division Series before Justice homered twice in the six-game ouster of Seattle that clinched the Yanks' third straight AL pennant. In New York City's first Subway Series since 1956, the Yankees easily beat the Mets in five games. "The wildest thing," Justice recalled, laughing, "was that you didn't have to get on a plane."

He did the next season, when the Yankees—in their post-9/11 sorrow—started the World Series in Arizona. "I thought we had that one," Justice said of a dramatic Game 7. "You've got Mariano Rivera on the mound in the ninth inning, you think, 'We've got it won.'" Yet even Rivera, the game's greatest closer, proved human that night. Once Rivera gave up the tying run, once Luis Gonzalez later looped a single to deny the Yankees a fourth consecutive world championship, Justice's World Series days were finally done.

"In Game 7, I got a hit, and they pinch-ran for me," he remembered. "When it was over, I looked up and thought, 'Let's put this on a larger scale.' Okay, Arizona had never won a championship. Curt Schilling had never won a championship. Randy Johnson had never won a championship. Why shouldn't those guys win a championship, too? They're two of the greatest pitchers of our time.

"So, I just went home."

His home away from home, however, would surely change yet again. This, Justice knew. "I knew I was going to be traded after that year," he said. "I was hurt, had an up-and-down year. I knew they'd make a change. But by that time, it was all business." A month later, the Yankees were open for business when they traded Justice to another borough: to Queens, and the Mets. A week later, however, the Mets dealt Justice to Oakland for Mark Guthrie and Tyler Yates.

"[Playing for Oakland] was a lot of fun," said Justice, who hit 11 home runs that 14th and final season to not only help the A's advance to another postseason, but to also finish his career with 305 homers and 1,017 RBIs. When Oakland lost the Division Series to Minnesota in five games, Justice thought, "Well, this is it for me. Time to go home."

This time it was for good. He was 36, happily remarried, and a father of three young children. It was time. "My whole thing was, I'd played long enough, had won a championship," Justice said. "I'd won a lot of personal rewards. And I didn't want to miss any of those things fathers can miss." So David Justice walked away with his health, happiness, family, and legacy intact. He's now a broadcaster for the Yankees' YES network, and resides in San Diego where the weather never varies and life is very, very good.

GAME OF MY LIFE

"In 1995, there was pressure. We *have* to win this World Series. They're starting to compare us to the Buffalo Bills. That's not sitting well with us at all.

"Games 1 and 2 of the Series are at our place. It's almost like a tennis match. So quiet. Our fans are spoiled. In Cleveland for Games 3, 4, and 5, the crowd was wild, like our fans were in '91.

"The day before Game 6, we're back in Atlanta for a workout day. Some reporters come to me and say, 'Orel Hershiser said all the pressure's on them.' On us—the Braves. I'm thinking he's playing mind games. So I said, 'You tell Orel Hershiser I said 'F-him, and if he wants some of me, come get some of me.'

"Then Omar Vizquel says, 'The Braves can't win a World Series. They've already lost two.' I said, 'Oh no-no-no-no-no.'

"I don't know how I got in this fuss, but my point was, our fans need to root for us. In Cleveland, they were doing all this stuff, going wild. And I *never* said our fans were horrible. Never. I said, 'They'll burn our houses down if we don't win'? Come on. And, 'If we get down 1-0, they'll probably boo us out of the stadium.'

"The next morning, I see the headlines. I said, 'Oh, man. Now the *Atlanta Journal-Constitution* can play that up. They can get me.' So it's not me against Hershiser. Or me versus Vizquel. No, [the *Journal-Constitution*] tried to put me against the fans. It's my fault that I said it, but the paper played it up.

"I come out on the field before the game, people are booing. They've all come out that night to watch me fail. I'm in the on-deck circle and I remember thinking, 'God, you've put me in a lot of tough positions and you've always brought me out of them. Please bring me out of this.'

"The next pitch, they announce my name—and the crowd's booing me. But I heard a few people cheering. And I said to myself, 'Okay, I'm playing for them.' I didn't make an out that night. I walked, got a double, a homer, and walked again. From that day on, I've seen God's power or God's hand on me as I walked through life.

"In the bottom of the fifth, Fred McGriff swings at three straight curveballs that all would've been balls. He struck out. When I got up in the sixth inning, I'm thinking, 'I'm gonna make this guy throw curves for strikes.' I didn't know [reliever] Jim Poole [who came on in the fifth inning]. But all pitchers throw fastballs.

"I started off 0-1, a fastball away, called a strike. Then it was 1-1; he tried to go fastball outside again, but this one was a ball. On the 1-1, I thought, 'Okay, this is a curveball count, but I'm gonna stay on the fastball.' The next pitch was a fastball inside. Home run. As soon as I hit it, I knew it was a home run.

"I'm rounding the bases, I'm thinking, 'We're about to blow open this game.' I hear all those people cheering. I let out the emotion. But my emotion is, 'Shut up. I don't want you cheering me. Keep on booing. This is about me and my teammates, our manager and coaches. And those few people who were cheering me at the start.'

"We go to the ninth inning. Glavine's pitched great; only gave up one hit. Now Wohlers is on in the ninth. We've lost two World Series. I'm thinking, 'Oh, if we get Kenny Lofton out, we're gonna win the World Series.' If Kenny gets on base, he's gonna steal second and just might steal third. What happens? Kenny fouls out to Pac Man [shortstop Rafael Belliard]. Omar Vizquel makes an out. And when [Carlos] Baerga hit it, I thought, 'Oh my God!' I thought it was out. But then I watched Marquis circle and catch that ball! I knew it was over. Oh, man!

"It was like the weight of the world was off of our shoulders. We'd finally won the World Series! And it was the first championship ever in Atlanta. You dream about winning the World Series. There's just not a better feeling."

Chapter 2

BOB HORNER

Has it been 20 years now? And at the time, did it all really last less than a decade?

Who else could shoehorn so much into nine seasons—from a star-studded big-league debut by a kid too young to drink, through a career chockablock with majestic homers, nasty contract disputes, nagging and disabling injuries, weight clauses, and good-gosh-almighty talent, and one historic, one-man home-run derby?

Who else but Bob Horner?

"Oh, God," Horner says now, in the familiar high-pitched, convivial voice that sounds too young for a guy pushing 50. "I don't think you can nail it all down to one thought or one meaning. There was just a lot going on—good and bad.

"But you take the good with the bad."

There was always a lot going on with Bob Horner, some remarkably good, some frustratingly bad, all of it memorable. And you took the good with the bad: the 215 homers he hit for Atlanta, including four on one memorable summer Sunday in 1986; the 380 games Horner missed during his nine years with the Braves; the prolonged stretches of brilliance by a kid who was the national college player of the year and the National League Rookie of the Year, all in the same year; the off-field contract disputes and collusion and injuries that included a twice-broken right wrist, which only added injury to insult. That was all part of the package that was James Robert Horner, who went from Junction City, Kansas, to Arizona State to the College World Series to becoming the No. 1 overall pick in the 1978 baseball draft. He promptly skipped the minors completely, became Atlanta's starting third baseman, and, in his first major-league game, homered off 286-game winner Bert Blyleven.

And then speaking of that feat afterward, Horner referred to the pitcher as "Mr. Blyleven."

"Absolutely," Horner says now when questioned about the formality and respect he showed for the veteran he took deep. "I'm 20 years old. I wasn't old enough to drink alcohol. The whole world was 'Mr.' to me."

The whole world was at his feet, too, in the summer of '78. The previous year, as a sophomore third baseman at Arizona State, Horner led the Sun Devils to the College World Series championship and was chosen the CWS Most Valuable Player. In 1978, he was named the national collegiate player of the year. Picked first in the MLB draft, Horner and his agent, Bucky Woy, not only cajoled a $175,000 signing bonus out of the Braves, but an immediate spot in the starting lineup, too. Forget getting seasoning at Double-A Savannah. After being drafted, Horner came to Atlanta-Fulton County Stadium to negotiate and sign a contract. He also got an up-close view of such big-league stars as Johnny Bench and George Foster of the Cincinnati Reds. Otherworldly in appearances on TV, in person they looked to Horner, "Just like me."

He signed a contract that June 14, and four days later made his big-league debut against Pittsburgh. By then, Horner and Woy had convinced Atlanta general manager Bill Lucas to let him break in at the top.

"The Braves didn't have a very good ballclub," Horner said. "I was just being honest. We kicked around the idea of starting at the major-

league level, with the proviso that, 'What's the worst that can happen?' If I don't do well, they can send me down.

"I think it took Bill by surprise; it had never really been done before," he said. "But the more you looked at the situation: 'Hey, they're right.'"

Today, the day and night of June 18 remains hazy for Horner: "I remember it just being a blur. I remember going to the clubhouse that afternoon and trying somehow to meet my teammates: Phil Niekro, Jeff Burroughs, Gary Mathews. I felt like a duck out of water.

"Then I remember being absolutely scared to death of going on the field," he said. "I had to calm down. My first at-bat was either a weak fly or a groundout. But I felt almost a moral victory, that I'd put the ball in play."

In his third at-bat, however, Horner took Mr. Blyleven deep for his first major-league homer. "Another Harmon Killebrew," was Montreal manager Dick Williams' assessment of Horner later that summer. Unlike the crewcut Killebrew, Horner had a mop of curly blond hair. But he, too, was a stocky third baseman with awesome power. In just 89 games that season, Horner smacked 23 home runs. His ratio of one homer every 14.04 at-bats was the best ever by a Rookie of the Year. In easily winning the NL award, Horner became the first player ever chosen as the College Player of the Year [after hitting a then-record 25 homers that season] and a major-league Rookie of the Year in the same season.

As for 1979? Let the contract disputes begin. Woy and Horner wanted a three-year, $1 million contract, an enormous pact for a second-year player in that era. Woy threatened filing a grievance for free agency, due to a contract technicality. Management and player-agent negotiated that winter in the newspapers. At one point, Woy said the Braves reneged on a contract agreement; Horner demanded a trade. Club owner Ted Turner—who'd once said, "Bob Horner is ready for stardom: Cooperstown"—went Teddy ballistic.

"If his spirit is broken, maybe we'll let him build it back up with some time in the minors," Turner threatened in the press that winter. ". . . His spirit is broken because we're only offering $100,000. I'll give him $300,000 when he deserves it. The only way I'll give him $300,000 this year is if he can make that cute blond hair curl without going to a hairdresser to get a permanent. A freshman in college doesn't run the family."

Woy and Horner reacted predictably: Indignantly. Bottom line: A contract was signed, and Horner played in Atlanta through 1986. Not without more contractual wrangling, however.

"That was a bad situation that just got worse," Horner said of the '79 contract impasse. "Bad because of the timing. We didn't have a very good year, to say the least. We finished last. Me, at 20 years old, I'm listening to the best advice and I'm not old enough to know what the best decision is.

"A lot of people so young, at 20 years old, are cast into making decisions that normally people 40 or 50 would have to make," he said. "I remember when our youngest son, Trent, turned 20, my wife, Chris, and I said, 'Can you imagine *him* being in the big leagues?

"I stand behind what we did, but things could've been done differently," Horner said. "It just got to be a big damn mess. It was just our fault, partly the Braves' fault, too. It was a stupid situation that never should've happened. It left a bad taste in a lot of people's mouths, and a taste that didn't go away for some for a long time."

In the off-season after his rookie year, Horner had his first surgery (on his left shoulder) as a Brave, then was beset by bone chips during the '79 campaign. Goodbye, Mr. Chips: Horner missed six weeks that season. Still, he batted .314 with a .552 slugging percentage; clobbered 33 home runs—fourth-best in the National League—in just 121 games; and drove in 98 runs.

If 1980 was again injury-plagued, it was also boffo again for Horner—despite Turner's attempt to demote him. After hitting just .059 in the first 10 games, Horner felt the owner's displeasure; Turner wanted to send Horner to Triple-A Richmond. When Horner refused to report, he was suspended and missed a couple of weeks. No matter: In just 124 games, Horner still belted 35 homers; 14 came in July, one shy of the big-league record held by Joe DiMaggio, Hank Greenberg, and ex-Brave Joe Adcock. In the strike-shortened 1981 season, Horner only played in 79 of 106 games, but still led Atlanta with 15 homers.

One of them was the 100th of his young career, at age 24, coming off Nolan Ryan.

Then came 1982, and much changed: Despite going 81-80, manager Bobby Cox was fired and replaced by ex-Brave Joe Torre. For much of that starry season, Horner stayed healthy.

"I remember just getting off to an unbelievable start," he said of Atlanta's record 13-0 start under Torre. "It really, really propelled us to where we ended up. We got such a jump on everybody; it takes the whole season to try to make that up."

The city, meanwhile, starved for a winner, went uncivilly mad.

"Let's face it: we hadn't really won," Horner said. "It had been 13 years since we'd won [the NL West]. So it was a galvanizing thing for the city of Atlanta. It was just like somebody turned a light switch on, and the people of Atlanta went nuts."

So did Horner, named to the NL All-Star team for the first and only time of his career, and now hitting behind the Braves' other young slugger, outfielder Dale Murphy.

"I had a lunch with Joe Torre after he took the job, and he told me he wanted me to hit behind Dale," Horner recalled. "Whether that meant me hitting fourth, third, sixth, fifth. And let's face it, it worked out."

Horner was on pace for career highs in homers and RBIs until a hyperextended elbow in mid-September caused him to miss the last two weeks of the regular season. Still, he finished with 32 home runs and 97 RBIs. Murphy, meanwhile, was a revelation with 36 homers, an NL-leading 109 runs batted in, his first Gold Glove, and a runaway win as the National League MVP. Atlanta edged out the Dodgers for the NL West title, only to be swept 3-0 by St. Louis in the National League Championship Series.

The following year, Murphy was even better (36 homers, 121 RBIs, .302 average, a second Gold Glove) and repeated as the most valuable player.

"Dale had some great years," Horner said. "I pray that he gets in the Hall of Fame. If you put Dale's numbers up against Kirby Puckett and Joe Carter, his numbers are very, very favorable. And if you look at their careers and MVP awards, too. Unfortunately, Dale never won a World Series championship.

"You wonder about that," he said. "But being an athlete, you can't change who you play for. That's not your fault. It's the hand you're dealt. Some players over the years get short-sheeted."

In 1983, Horner was hit by injuries again: A bum ankle caused him to sit out 10 games in June, then a broken navicular bone in his right wrist cost him the last seven weeks of the season.

"It never really healed. I spent a year rehabbing it," said Horner, who broke the wrist again on May 30 of the following year, and missed the rest of the season. "Some people are blessed with [health]—well, like a Nolan Ryan, who's pitched forever and still threw hard 'til the day he quit. I hurt my left shoulder in college, the year I was drafted. Medicine and surgical procedures were not as advanced back then.

"My shoulder was the type of injury that was going to plague me forever," he said. "And then I broke the wrist. It's all going to drag you down. I felt like a cripple."

At times in his career, Horner—who is 6-foot-1, and whose listed, ideal playing weight was 215—had weight clauses in his contract. He says now he didn't mind them at all.

"Joe Torre came in as manager; he was a catcher and was a heavy player," Horner said. "Then he lost a bunch of weight and won the MVP. He was absolutely sold on this. He came to Atlanta and said to me, in public and in private, 'I think you have a body type like I had. If there was a chance I didn't watch it, you can balloon up.

"Joe said, 'If you stay below 215, you get a bonus,'" Horner said. "I thought, 'Hey, why the hell not?'"

Despite that second wrist surgery, Horner reported early to spring training in '85, started on Opening Day, but also carefully monitored his wrist. Still, the kid hit. Oh, how he could hit. Despite resting periodically early in the season, Horner played a career-high 130 games, and, midway through the season, switched to first base. The following season, his numbers were even better: a new career-best of 141 games; 27 homers, good for fifth in the NL; and 87 RBIs (ninth). For the seventh time in nine major-league seasons, Horner had hit 20 or more homers.

Five of those 1986 blasts were very significant. On June 19, Horner hit his 200th career home run. July 6, 1986, however, is the date circled in red on Horner's historical calendar. The day he made baseball history in Atlanta-Fulton County Stadium by hitting four home runs in a game against the Montreal Expos. To this day, a middle-aged Braves fan still rues the fact that he missed two of Horner's four home runs. It was a hot Atlanta afternoon, and the beer must have been especially cold and inviting. For two of Horner's homers, the fan was stuck in the men's room at the ballpark.

GAME OF MY LIFE

"I'd hit three homers in a game in college. I'd hit two in a game with the Braves. But never four.

"What I remember about it is, every time I came up we were losing. We lost the game, 11-9. It was a Sunday getaway game in Atlanta. We were taking off afterward, going to Philadelphia.

"[Each of my home runs] were just pitchers making mistakes—hanging breaking balls—more than [anything I did]. But they could afford to make them; they were ahead. They kept throwing 'em, and I kept hitting 'em. And we lost.

"The first three homers, off Andy McGaffigan, were hanging breaking balls. Hanging breaking balls are mistakes. You're not always going to get great pitches to hit. You might get one great pitch to hit an at-bat. That day, I hit mistakes.

"I don't know if I'd ever faced McGaffigan before. I didn't know much about him. He didn't know much about me.

"I don't think any of the home runs I hit even tied [the game], much less put us ahead. I hit three in a row, my first three at-bats. All four were to left field, or left-center. But after the first three off McGaffigan, another pitcher—a sinkerballer [Tim Burke]—came in. He broke my bat. I popped out to first base.

"Jeff Reardon came in in the bottom of the eighth. We were losing 11-7 [in the bottom of the ninth], with two out [when I came to the plate again]. Jeff's a fastball pitcher. He threw it and I hit it. Jeff got the save and won the game. He didn't mind. He didn't lose a minute's sleep over it. McGaffigan and I never talked about it. Our paths never crossed.

"It was a strange day. Yeah, I'd done it. It was a wonderful feeling. But it's a team game, in a team sport, and there wasn't much to celebrate about because we lost. After the game, we showered and packed and boarded the bus and flew to Philadelphia.

"When you get your butt kicked, there's not much to celebrate.

"I have both my bats and the [last] ball from that game. I hit the first three homers with one bat. I gave that one to Cooperstown. The bat I hit the fourth home run with, I have. I liked it so much, I kept using it. I used it until I broke it. Then I taped it up and hung onto it.

"Either a fan, or a member of the grounds crew got the fourth [home run] ball for me. About five years ago or so, I donated the bat and that ball to the Braves Museum and Hall of Fame at Turner Field. I figure it'd be better to have it there. It was just sitting here gathering dust in my house. I figured someone might enjoy it, and remember the day.

"It's been a really fun thing. People coming up to me and saying, 'Hey, I was at the game!' Or writing me a note about it. It's been really nice."

✳ ✳ ✳

Surely, that day is a much nicer memory for Horner than the following off-season. The road to Tokyo, Japan and the Yakult Swallows in the spring of '87 was not an easy path, nor one Horner had ever anticipated needing to travel.

"It was unfortunate in that I'd played 10 years [actually nine at that point] in the big leagues," said Horner. "That's what I wanted to do, keep playing here. No knock on the Japanese, but I wanted to stay here.

"Unfortunately, that's when collusion [by the owners] came in, and the Braves offered me a 75 percent pay cut," he said. "You went around the league, and people wouldn't offer [big] money. You had guys like Andre Dawson, Lance Parrish, Tim Raines, who were free agents. Andre Dawson was probably the best of the best then, and you wonder, 'What's up?' And you scratch your head. But you know what's going on."

Christmas came and went. New Year's, too. All Horner had on the table was that slashed-salary offer from Atlanta. Not a word from any other team.

"It's January, and I haven't heard from anybody," he said. "I don't know what to do. I'm working out trying to keep myself in shape. Out of nowhere, the Japanese call and say, 'What do you think?'

"I said, 'About what?' They said, 'About coming over here and playing?'

"I can't imagine not playing that year," Horner recalled. "I'm 29 years old. I finally came to the realization that I had to do it—play over there."

So he swallowed hard and signed a one-year, $1.3-million contract (including travel and living expenses) with the Yakult Swallows of the Japan Central League. Ownership predicted Horner would hit 50 homers. Indeed, six of his first seven hits were home runs—one in his first game, three in the second. He finished with 31 [in just 303 at-bats, an average of one every 9.8 at-bats], and hit .327.

When he returned to the U.S. the following year, Horner told reporters of his time in Japan, "I don't have any funny anecdotes. Life last year was not amusing." From a distance of nearly two decades, Horner now reflects in a different light.

"The Japanese were marvelous," he said. "Wonderful hosts. Wonderful to my family. The [players] were great. My sons [Tyler and Trent] lived in another country for six months.

"At the time, I felt like I was in the wrong place at the wrong time," Horner said. "I enjoyed being there; I just wish I could've made the decision to be here."

Following that initial season, Yakult offered a $10-million contract over three years, but Horner returned to the U.S., primarily for family considerations. When slugging first baseman/free agent Jack Clark left St. Louis for the New York Yankees, Horner and Woy contacted Cardinals management. Manager Whitey Herzog's initial response: "I don't want Horner." Upper management did, however, and offered Horner a one-year, $950,000 contract with a $500,000 bonus if he played at least 135 games.

Horner didn't make even half that number. "We got off to a good start, but I blew out my shoulder for the fourth time," said Horner, who played just 60 games in 1988 and hit but three homers. "I had arthroscopic surgery. Then I went to Los Angeles to see [noted orthopedic surgeon] Dr. Frank Jobe." Horner underwent another shoulder surgery that August 6, his 31st birthday. The following spring, he tried to catch on, to hold onto baseball, this time in spring training camp with the Baltimore Orioles. "It just wasn't there," Horner remembered. "I'd lost so much muscle tone, and there was the surgery. Dr. Jobe had told me after the surgery that there was a lot of muscle damage: 'This might work, it might not.'"

It didn't work. That spring, Horner recalls flying back to Miami, the O's spring training headquarters, from a players' association meeting.

"I was the National League player rep then, and on the flight back to Miami it was just a feeling of helplessness," Horner said. "You're going down in a pool and you can't stop it. So you just let go. My shoulder was killing me."

After landing, Horner went to see Roland Hemond, then the general manager of the Orioles. "I told him, 'You need to give this [roster] spot to a young kid who can help you. I can make the team, but I can't help you,'" Horner recalled.

Today he remembers the moment distinctly: "It was a terrible day."

✳ ✳ ✳

From a distance—Horner has lived in the Las Colinas area of Dallas for more than two decades—his view of the Braves, and his perspective on them, is clear.

"It's incredible," Horner said of the club's 14-year string of division titles that finally ended last fall. "It truly is incredible. When you think about what they've accomplished. . . . And the criticism is, 'Well, they only won one World Series.'

"It's the team that gets to the playoffs that's hot that wins," he said. "But the accomplishment of winning 14 in a row, that will never, *never* happen again. I give Bobby Cox huge kudos for that, also John Schuerholz, the architect behind it."

And as for Horner, now on the cusp of his 50th birthday? "I'm not really doing anything now," he said, chuckling. "I'm playing some golf. Both of the boys graduated from college and are working and doing well.

"It was a fun life," Horner said of his baseball career. "It was a fun career. And I have a good life."

Chapter 3

MARK LEMKE

It's been 16 seasons now since baseball was formally introduced to a little switch-hitting second baseman: Mark Lemke, who eventually and unexpectedly became, as an *Atlanta Journal-Constitution* headline cried, "ReMARKable!"

"It seems forever since '91," said Lemke. "But it also seems like yesterday. Really, the numbers are harder for me to compute, until I look at it like a little kid."

That's essentially what he was: A little kid, a 5-foot-9, 167-pound backup second baseman, until regular Jeff Treadway was hurt in September of 1991. Then Lemke took over. He helped the Braves overtake Los Angeles to win the National League West, then fashioned a postseason most little kids only dream of.

"That year, '91, I don't think will ever be duplicated," Lemke said of the Braves' sudden ascendance. "Especially not in the Atlanta Braves' history."

In Atlanta's unlikely worst-to-first run, Lemke was the unlikeliest of heroes. "Lemmer," his teammates called him. Or, "Scoots." As in, "You know, how Lemmer always scoots around the field."

"The original dirt player," manager Bobby Cox labeled Lemke. Like Pigpen of Charles Schulz's *Peanuts* cartoon fame, Lemke always seemed to play amidst a cloud of dust. In that star-kissed autumn of '91, his dust was golden.

Even after the Braves had added Terry Pendleton, Sid Bream, and Rafael Belliard in the previous off-season, much of the '91 ballclub remained homegrown. In the minors, Lemke remembers "me and 'Blaus,'" shortstop Jeff Blauser, then his best friend, sitting on a park bench one night during spring training, with no car and nothing to do, trying to imagine what the future held for them.

For two good buddies, the future was "Wow!" In Game 2 of the '91 National League Championship Series in Pittsburgh, Lemke doubled in the game's only run. He then saved that crucial 1-0 victory with a diving stop of an eighth-inning, up-the-middle grounder off the bat of Jay Bell. Lemke kept the ball in the infield, preventing the speedy Gary Redus from scoring the tying run.

After the Braves dropped Games 4 and 5 in Atlanta and returned to Pittsburgh in a 3-2 predicament, after Steve Avery and John Smoltz pitched superbly to win Games 6 and 7, Lemke recalled, "Ron Gant and I were on the plane, saying, 'We're not going home! We're going to Minnesota! We're going to the World Series!'"

Lemke didn't start that Series opener in Minneapolis, in the maelstrom of the Metrodome. "Which might've been good," Lemke said. "Maybe Bobby was taking my heartbeat. It was going so fast, to the point where it gives you amnesia.

"There's only a couple of things I remember."

Down 2-0, the Braves returned home to a civic embrace that had built throughout the pennant race, blossomed in the NLCS, and now raged into the World Series. "You really loved it," Lemke said. "In basketball, they call it the sixth man. In football, Texas A&M has the 12th man. In baseball, that's what the fans were like to me.

"It meant a lot, to have a full stadium," Lemke said. "The first game when I broke in [in a 1988 call-up], 3,500 people were in the stands."

Fast forward to 1991. Multiply that crowd by 16. Don't even try to count the decibels.

"In '91, I don't think you can ever duplicate that outpouring of affection," said Lemke. "I mean, man, everybody was into it. We'd go to the airport, and the chain gang dropped their tools and did the Tomahawk Chop when our buses drove by.

"They're probably ticked off at the world," he said, "and they turn and give you the Chop."

In turn, Lemke gave them all an October to remember, a World Series performance to never forget. His two-out single off Rick Aguilera in the 12th inning of Game 3 scored David Justice with the winning run in a 5-4, four-hour marathon. This, after Minnesota answered solo home runs by Justice and Lonnie Smith with homers by Kirby Puckett and Chili Davis. That tied it at four-all in the eighth, before Lemke's late-night heroics.

"Then, it was into La-La Land," Lemke said. "I went into an unconscious state of mind. I was in a zone. It was, like, 'Wow!'"

"Wow!" indeed. The following evening, in Game 4, Lemke tripled with one out in the ninth. When pinch-hitter Jerry Willard stepped into the batter's box, Lemke stood on third base, exhausted and thinking, "Just hit it deep enough."

At first, when Willard lofted a fly ball to right field, Lemke thought it had traveled much farther than it actually had. He waited, he recalled, for what seemed to be "an eternity" until the ball was caught. Then, after tagging up and taking off, Lemke took advantage of a throw to home that was "up the line a little bit." "The original dirt player" slid home safely in the dirt for a 3-2 victory and Atlanta's first-ever World Series win. The next night, Lemke tripled twice more in Game 5—his three triples tied a World Series record, and one of Lemke's bats eventually wound up in the Baseball Hall of Fame—as Atlanta won 14-5 to take a 3-2 lead.

In Minnesota, however, Puckett's 11th-inning homer off Charlie Leibrandt forced a decisive Game 7. When Jack Morris outlasted John

Smoltz in a magnificent pitching duel, his 10-inning, 1-0 masterpiece gave Minnesota the world championship. It also earned Morris the most valuable player award. If not, Lemke would surely have been the MVP. He hit .417 for the Series, the highest average on either team, and led the Braves with a .708 slugging percentage.

"As a player, you always play to win," Lemke said. "So '95 [when Atlanta beat Cleveland to finally win the World Series] will always go down as No. 1, but it will never compare to '91. Never."

Lemke became the regular second baseman in 1992. Although he batted just .227, Cox loved Lemke's defense. The manager truly appreciated the Lemmer's team-high .333 average in the '92 NCLS when Atlanta stunned Pittsburgh 3-2 on Francisco Cabrera's two-out, two-run single in the bottom of the ninth of Game 7.

"That was the only year that I felt we got beat in the four World Series I played in," Lemke said. "We could've won in '91. We could've, and should've, won in '96 against the Yankees. In '95, we did win. But in '92, Toronto flat-out beat us."

In the strike-shortened 1994 season, Lemke hit a career-high .294. His .994 fielding percentage broke a franchise record for second basemen that had stood for 32 years. By 1997, though, Lemke was suffering vision problems that ultimately ended his career.

"Little blind spots in my right eye," he said. "I still have problems today looking at a computer."

After signing with Boston in 1998, Lemke played just 17 games for the Red Sox before a concussion ended his season. That, and vision problems, ended his career. He considered trying to make a comeback as a pitcher after fooling around with a knuckleball with an independent minor-league team in Montclair, New Jersey. Wisely, Lemke thought better of that.

Today he still lives in the Atlanta area, invests in real estate, and is part-owner of a baseball school in suburban Duluth. Lemke now does pre- and postgame work on Braves radio broadcasts. He'll never be mistaken for Pete Van Wieren or Skip Caray. No matter. He's miles away from the kid second baseman of the late '80s.

"In 1988, we lost 106 games," Lemke said. "In '89 and '90, we lost 97 games each year. And in '91? Bam! I love Chipper and Andruw and all those guys, but I'm glad I got to see both sides. They've only seen the winning side [until 2006].

"In '91, I don't think we were as talented as the latter [Braves championship] teams," Lemke said. "We were molded by chemistry, and kind of plugged the holes. We weren't like the Yankees.

"Later, it seemed every year there was a Javy Lopez, a Chipper Jones, or an Andruw Jones coming up," he said. "And your new guy on the team [eventually becomes] a $100-million player—and it didn't cost you anything, 'cause they were in the organization."

Yet none of them ever had an October quite like Lemke's memorable month in '91. That classic fall when he became the most unlikely Braves hero of all.

GAME OF MY LIFE

"In the '91 World Series, everything seemed to fall into place. It seemed everything I wanted was coming our way. If I wanted a fastball right here, there it was.

"I think if one game in my career stands out for me, it'd be Game 3 of that World Series. It was such an emotional turn for us, and also myself. It was my first World Series victory—Atlanta's first World Series victory. And I'd made an error earlier in the game, and we were already down two games to none. It was a routine double-play ball, and it got by me. I overran the ball. I don't know how. Chuck Knoblauch hit a grounder, and it was going toward right field. I ran toward first base and ran right past it. That loaded the bases with nobody out.

"I remember feeling terrible. I was young, and I got an opportunity to play in a World Series, on the biggest stage. And then that happens. That felt like the bottom of the world. I remember the guys huddling around me on the mound, Terry Pendleton and Sid Bream and Greg Olson. They were saying, 'Hey, we're going to get you out of this situation and pick you up.' And I was definitely thinking, like, 'We'll be Houdini if we can get out of this.'

"But we did get out of it, with a strikeout and a double play. Then things changed in about an hour. In the dugout, Olson said to me, 'You're gonna win it for us.' And I'm thinking, 'Yeah, right.'

"In the 12th inning, I remember it was going to be a tough at-bat against Rick Aguilera. He had good command and great movement on his ball. A real good sinker. I wanted to get a pitch up. I didn't want to have to face his split-finger [fastball]. I don't remember the count. I do remember not thinking about what Greg Olson had said, although he'd reminded me in the dugout. But I singled with two outs and Dave Justice scored the winning run from second.

"That was the first World Series win for the Atlanta Braves, and it meant a lot to me. . . . Even though we didn't win the World Series, without that [Game 3-winning hit] it wouldn't have been as dramatic a Series.

"Those were long, long days. It wasn't just the fatigue, the physical tiredness I felt. It was the tension, too, building all day and then during those [grueling, close] games."

✳ ✳ ✳

As a kid, Mark Lemke was told early on that the closest he'd ever get to the Baseball Hall of Fame was Utica, his hometown in upstate New York, which may be best known as the home of the second-oldest beer brewer in the nation, F.X. Matt Brewing Company. Growing up, Lemke regularly went to Cooperstown for the hall's annual induction weekend exhibition game. One summer, little boy Lemke—who couldn't get a ticket—stood outside the ballpark, beyond the right-field fence.

"They had a short porch," recalled Lemke. On that day, such ball field dimensions played to his favor. Pittsburgh's Manny Sanguillen smacked a homer over that short porch, and Lemke chased the ball, running through a small stand of trees and diving to the ground to snag his memento. Come 1991, he created his own memories, ones to last a lifetime.

In hindsight, Lemke's lament in the immediate aftermath of Game 7 of that epic Fall Classic seems shortsighted, if justifiably so. "You wonder if you'll ever get that chance again, if you let something slip through your fingers forever," he says now.

When an official from the Baseball Hall of Fame approached him in the Metrodome clubhouse, Lemke wondered, "What could he possibly want?" The guy wanted the Lemmer's bat; after all, he'd tied a World Series record with three triples. At first, Lemke demurred. He wanted to keep the bat for his personal collection of memorabilia. Then, Lemke realized the Hall of Fame is just 45 minutes from Utica. "So I could go visit it," he said. Today, it's still a thrill for Lemke that his bat, something of his very own and symbolic of that miraculous 1991 season, is a part of Cooperstown lore.

Chapter 4

ALBERT HALL

Sometimes, even a nondescript player can suddenly, unexpectedly, astonishingly leave his mark on the game of baseball. Exhibit A: Albert Hall.

In the midst of one of the most forlorn periods in Braves history, in an otherwise meaningless late-season game in September of 1987, Hall achieved what Hank Aaron could not. Or Eddie Mathews. Or Dale Murphy. Or either of the Joneses, Chipper or Andruw. Against the Houston Astros in the last week of that abominable '87 season, in which the Braves lost 92 games under skipper Chuck Tanner, Hall somehow fashioned a baseball—and certainly a Braves—rarity: He hit for the cycle, a feat that's statistically even rarer than pitching a no-hitter, yet one far less acclaimed.

Against the Astros on the evening of September 23, Hall recorded a single, double, triple, and home run in the same game. In a 5-4 Atlanta victory, the switch-hitting center fielder also scored the tying and winning runs. Imagine that: Albert Hall and the cycle, in the same sentence. In the Braves franchise record book. Now we know how many hits it takes to fill the Albert Hall scrapbook of major-league mementoes: four.

"Count me in," Hall said that night. "It was exciting, especially because it was in the major leagues."

Hall had hit for the cycle as a minor-leaguer in 1982, while playing for Atlanta's Triple-A affiliate in Richmond. His major-league cycle, however, was a real rarity. How rare? It was just the fourth cycle in Braves history, and the first in 77 years. Bill Collins, a rookie and, like Hall, a little-known outfielder, hit for the cycle as a Boston Brave in 1910. That was the third cycle in franchise history, following Duff Cooley (1904) and John Bates (1907). Hall's was No. 4.

Now, 20 years later, fully 96 seasons since Bill Collins' cycle and despite the club's great run since '91, the Braves are still waiting for No. 5.

✳ ✳ ✳

"I don't remember everything," Hall said of his baseball career, which began back in Birmingham, Alabama, where Hall was born and raised and has lived since his career ended in 1989 following a late-season call-up by the Pittsburgh Pirates. "They had Lonnie Smith come in that year [1988]," Hall said of the one-time All-Star outfielder who played sparingly in '88 but rediscovered his early '80s stroke to hit .315 in 1989. "The axe is just part of it. Everybody gets the axe, sometime or other."

Smith's resurgence ended a nine-year big-league sojourn for Hall that included brief September cups of call-up coffee in 1981, '82 and '83, five seasons in the major leagues with Atlanta, his release by the Braves, and an '89 season spent mostly with Pittsburgh's Triple-A club in Buffalo before a very brief September call-up. And then came Hall's departure from the game.

"I just remember being up there, and seeing the maturity of guys, seeing the talent," said Hall, 49, who has worked for a tubing products company since leaving baseball. "I remember the knowledge of the game, and then leaving it.

"Baseball is a funny game," he continued. "I've seen guys come up that try to figure it out. That's the biggest enemy. Just play the game."

In his day, that one singular sensation on a September night was the pinnacle of Hall's career. "Most people say the cycle was the biggest thing," he said. "I guess it was, but at the time, I didn't know it happened. If I'd seen me doing it, watched me hit a homer, single, double, and a triple, I'd have been more excited."

$$* * *$$

To go for the cycle requires hitting ability, speed, power, and, quite often, sheer good fortune. A single and a double are the easy parts. A player must be able to collect a triple as well as go deep for a homer. Amazingly, Albert Hall accomplished his cycle in the most difficult manner imaginable: He saved the toughest component of the cycle— legging out a triple—for his final at-bat in the ninth inning.

For Hall, though, that triple off Astros ace reliever Dave Smith in the ninth inning was his fourth of the season. It was his home run, however, that fairly astounded. In a nine-year major-league career, Hall hit just five homers in 772 at-bats, including three in that '87 season. The third of those home runs, off Houston starter Jim Deshaies, was a key ingredient in Hall's cycle. His fifth and final big-league homer would come in 1988, Hall's last season before retirement.

Yet Hall also hit just eight triples in his career. A lithe, light-hitting, switch-hitting outfielder with fine speed, Hall had just 196 hits in his major-league career. Only 47 were extra-base hits, 35 of them for doubles. Indeed, his cycle was one of the most harmonic of baseball convergences. Consider the only other major leaguers who hit for the cycle in 1987: Andre Dawson, Candy Maldonado, and Tim Raines. As they sing on *Sesame Street*, "One of these things is not like the other. One of these things does not belong."

Once, Atlanta had considered Hall a better big-league prospect than Brett Butler. The fleet outfielder (a four-time minor-league base-stealing champion in the Braves' farm system) had been forecast as the franchise's center fielder of the future. Yet Hall never played in more than 92 games in any season for Atlanta. He peaked in '87, posting that career high in games played as well as at-bats while stealing 33 bases. Matter of fact, that year Hall achieved another statistical obscurity in the Braves record book: he became the first Atlanta Brave with 30 or more steals while playing in fewer than 100 games.

"I've never quit on anything in my life," Hall, who was hitting .295 at the time, said immediately following his historic cycle. "I've been sent back to the minors, but I wasn't going to quit. I can't think about next year now. I have to finish strong and see what happens."

Instead, Hall slumped a bit but still finished with a .284 average that season. That was easily his highest in the big leagues—23 percentage points higher than his previous best of .261 in 1984, his first full season in Atlanta.

That memorable September night, however, Albert Hall was everything Atlanta had ever envisioned. He'd already singled and doubled by the time he faced Deshaies in the sixth. His two-out solo homer tied the game at 4-4. Come the ninth, he led off with a shot inside the first-base line. Hall had to avoid Astros first baseman Glenn Davis, who was blocking the basepath near the bag. He dodged Davis, then sped to third for a triple and a piece of history.

"I didn't know anything about it," he later said of his cycle. "I just heard people cheering and looked up at the board. I never even thought about it."

The scoreboard advised the fans of Hall's accomplishment. Hal Lanier, the Houston manager, did not exactly share their enthusiasm.

"A .240 hitter [Braves shortstop Jeff Blauser] wears us out last night, and now Albert Hall hits a homer," Lanier said after his tantrum in the visiting manager's office. "We're probably playing the worst of anybody in the league right now."

Hall, who finished the game four-of-five at the plate with two runs and a RBI, had never had such a night in the big leagues. Never would again, either.

GAME OF MY LIFE

"When I got to third base, [Braves third-base coach] Russ Nixon told me what I'd done. And it flashed up on the board: 'Albert Hall Hit for the Cycle.'

"Any four-hit game is great. A four- or five-hit game, with some RBIs, is a strong night. With a cycle, that's a really good night.

"After the triple, when they were flashing it up on the board, I got a standing ovation from the fans. The next day, Ted Turner told me, 'Great game.' It was a good feeling.

"The thing about Jim Deshaies was, I always [played against] him. I always faced the lefties when they came to town. The double, single, and home run came from the right-hand side [of the batter's box]. The triple came off the left-hand side, down the line into the right-field corner.

"The single and double were both [hit] to the left side [of the field]; the single up the middle, to the left side of second base, and the double to left-center. The home run had to be down the left-field line.

"Dave Smith was a great pitcher. I hit the triple on a slider. He threw a lot of sliders, hundreds of sliders. It's a good pitch. A good slider's hard to hit. You hit it, you foul it off your foot, or pull it foul. Or you get jammed. But if he misses his location with it, you can hit it. He just got it out over the plate a bit. Didn't get it in enough.

"The triple wasn't on the first pitch, although a lot of times I chased the first pitch 'cause they're usually fastballs. My biggest thing was to stay ahead of the pitcher, stay ahead in the count. I must've had a strike or so on me. You always get one pitch to hit. You just can't miss it. I didn't.

"Glenn Davis was at first base. First basemen are always on the runner when he's coming around, making sure he touched the base. He was just in the [basepath]. I didn't even have a certain foot I touched first base with. I cut it sharp, hit it with my left foot. When balls are [hit] in gaps, I always tried to touch the inside of the base with my left foot, to keep me from going out too far. [Davis impeded me] just a little bit, but not too much. He didn't want to get [called for] obstruction of the runner.

"But I still didn't know I was going for the cycle. I didn't have a clue—I was just running hard. You're always thinking 'double,' running hard on any ball hit to the outfield. When you hit a ball into the right-field corner, you take a peek [at it rounding first]. Then you're looking at the third-base coach, for the 'come on' sign. [I got it] and I slid headfirst into third.

"Right now, I look back at my career, and I don't care how many bad days I had. Every day was a good day—especially that one."

✳ ✳ ✳

Hall recalled that "a guy named Bill Collins" was the last Brave to hit for the cycle before he did so. Told that Collins accomplished that in 1910, Hall said, with a chuckle, "That was a long time ago!"

Hall's a bit surprised that it's been nearly 20 years since his feat and still no Brave has duplicated it. "The triple was the hard one to get," he said. "I'm sure some guys in Atlanta have come close, but they couldn't get the triple.

"A lot of times, guys that are [good] average hitters—spray the ball hitters—have a chance to get the cycle," Hall said. "Chipper could do it, guys that hit for average. Andruw could do it, too. He's got the legs. If he hit more to the opposite field, if he sprayed the ball around the field, he could do it.

"You've got to learn to hit the gaps, and the corners," he said. "And if you're blessed with a good pair of legs, use 'em."

Except for the occasional summer softball games at New Mt. Zion Baptist Church, Hall doesn't play the game anymore. He still loves it, though. Misses baseball, too. Always will.

"That's something that will never leave [me]," Hall said. "I don't think there's a [retired] ballplayer that's still not got it in him. It's something great to do—to play. I miss it."

Hall played in a Braves-related charity golf tournament last summer. Last September, he signed autographs in the plaza at Turner Field before a Braves-Marlins Sunday matinee, then watched the game with his wife, Suzette, and son, Albert.

He followed the Braves' 14-year reign as division champions, like Braves fans everywhere. "They had great years," Hall said. "The year they won the World Series [1995], they were really great. They could've won more, too. They just had bad breaks. It could've happened, but it seemed it just wasn't meant for them."

And as for his status as the last Brave to hit for the cycle? Does Albert Hall hope that endures?

"It's always good to continue to last," he said. "People still remind me of that. They're more happy for me than I am myself. You always hope that continues to last.

"As long as it lasts, there's a connection," Hall said. "People call me and they say, 'Al, I'm watching the Braves on TV and they're talking about you again!' It's always good. Good to be the answer to a trivia question."

Chapter 5

PHIL NIEKRO

Imagine if Primo hadn't hurt his pitching arm. That's what they called him: "Primo," the most popular of several monikers for Phil Niekro Sr., a strapping coal miner in the Ohio Valley town of Lansing, Ohio. He was also a sandlot pitcher in an industrial league on weekends, a 6-foot-2, 220-pounder who fired a 90 mph fastball.

At least until the day Primo hurt his arm and lost his heater. Not to worry: Another coal miner, Nick McKay, a self-taught knuckleballer himself, showed Primo how to throw the knuckler and fool batters with butterflies, not bullets. Primo, in turn, shared the secrets of the knuckleball with his boys: first his older son, Phil, then the younger son, Joe.

And wouldn't the history of the Atlanta Braves be different if Primo hadn't?

"I'd probably have wound up a coal miner, like my Dad," Niekro said. "Either that, or a steelworker. Or a game warden. I grew up fishing, hunting, just outside all the time."

As Niekro spoke, he was sitting and sipping inside Common Grounds, a funky coffee shop on Main Street in Flowery Branch. The little hamlet an hour north of Atlanta is best known as the headquarters and practice facility of the NFL's Atlanta Falcons. For Niekro, its proximity to Lake Lanier is far more important than how close it is to Michael Vick's personal playground.

"I still fish," said Niekro, who lives with his wife, Nancy, in their gorgeous home near the Flowery Branch marina. "But I'm slowing down. I don't get out more than twice a day now."

Primo's oldest boy smiled. He smiles a lot. You would, too, if you were Phil Niekro, for whom life is still good 20 years after he retired from baseball, nearly a decade since his induction into the Baseball Hall of Fame. He is still one of the most popular Atlanta Braves of all time. All because Primo hurt his pitching arm and his namesake learned how to fluster hitters with the dancing pitch.

But then, what else would you expect from a pitcher who was born in 1939 on April Fool's Day? Follow the bouncing ball? Good luck, fellas. And blame Nick McKay, 86 that August day in 1997 when, having ridden one of four buses packed with townsfolk from Lansing, McKay sat in the audience in Cooperstown, savoring the induction ceremonies and Niekro's entrance into the Hall of Fame. McKay was not alone. There were 35 members of the Braves 400 Club, the team's most faithful, longtime fan club in attendance that afternoon. Then-Georgia governor and then-Democrat Zell Miller was there, too, as well as "Uncle Ernie," ex-Boston and Milwaukee Braves pitcher and Atlanta Braves broadcaster Ernie Johnson Sr. and Bob Horner, the 1978 National League Rookie of the Year.

"Phil," Horner said that Sunday in Cooperstown, "was the greatest teammate you could ever have."

Almost every Atlanta teammate of Niekro's echoes Horner's sentiments. Yet Niekro was enshrined in Cooperstown for far more than just being a good guy. His statistics, accomplishments, and awards are staggering. In 24 big-league seasons, Niekro won 318 games. From 1967, his first full season with Atlanta, until the strike-shortened season of 1981, he had 14 consecutive seasons of 10 or more wins. Three of them were 20-win seasons, including a career-

high 23 in 1969, which stood as an Atlanta record until John Smoltz won 24 in 1996. Niekro pitched more than 300 innings four times, with a career-best 342 in 1979. From 1974-80, he led the National League in innings pitched four times and was never lower than fifth in that stretch. He pitched a no-hitter against San Diego on August 5, 1973. On October 6, 1987, he became the oldest pitcher—at age 46—to record a shutout with a four-hit, 8-0 victory over Toronto. He made five All-Star appearances (four as a Brave), won five Gold Gloves, pitched in two NLCS, and was then 14th on baseball's all-time win list when he retired with 318 victories. His Atlanta pitching records will surely never be broken: Most games (689), complete games (226), innings pitched (4,533), victories (266), strikeouts (2,855), shutouts (43), and hits allowed (4,136).

Niekro's number 35 was retired by the Braves while he was still active and pitching in the American League for the Yankees. He's enshrined in the Braves Hall of Fame. In 1977, he even struck out four Pirates—Dave Parker, Bill Robinson, Rennie Stennett, and Omar Moreno—in one inning, so nasty was the knuckleball that game it was nearly as uncatchable to the Braves catcher as it was unhittable to the batters. Niekro also won Major League Baseball's Lou Gehrig and Roberto Clemente Awards.

In short, not bad for a kid who was nearly released shortly after signing with the Braves for the princely signing bonus of $500. In 1959, Niekro—whose basketball teammate at Bridgeport High was John Havlicek, and who pitched in a high school game against Bill Mazeroski—turned down a college baseball scholarship to sign with the Milwaukee Braves. He took a train to spring training in Waycross, Georgia, and found himself among 300-400 young kids, all of whom thought they were pretty good ballplayers.

"I thought, 'Holy smokes, there's a lot of guys here!'" Niekro recalled. "I made friends, and talked to guys, and found out, 'Oh, he got $80,000 [as a signing bonus].' And $60,000, $40,000, $70,000. I thought, 'Holy smokes! These guys must be pretty good!'"

Niekro was assigned to the Braves' Wellsville, New York, affiliate, the lowest class in the club's organization. "I remember taking a bus—with no air conditioning—up to Wellsville," he said. "It was my first time away from home, from my parents. But it was the big leagues to me."

One day, Niekro arrived early at the ballpark. "I see a car parked on Main St., which is about as big as this," he said, looking out the coffee house window onto Main St. in Flowery Branch, which will never be confused with Peachtree Street in Atlanta. Niekro knew the driver looked familiar. "I recognized him from spring training," he said. "He was a big-bonus money guy. I thought, 'Oh, somebody's getting released today.'"

Once inside the clubhouse, Niekro was summoned by player-manager Harry Minor. "We're getting two new players," Minor told him. "The Braves are going to release you."

"The first thing I thought about was I'm gonna wind up like my dad in a coal mine," Niekro recalled. "Either that or a steel mill. I got this opportunity and I screwed it up. I sat there and said, 'I'm not going.'

"He said, 'You're going.' I cried my eyes out. I said, 'Hey, I'm not going!' I thought they were gonna call security. I said, 'Harry, I need to play. I need to play. I need to play!'"

Niekro refused to lose, or move for that matter. Minor relented. Sort of. He convinced the Braves organization to send Niekro to McCook, Nebraska, where the club had a team in a rookie league that was just starting play. Niekro agreed to go. He also agreed to stop crying. It took two days—by plane, then bus—to get to McCook. "I get there and go up to the hotel, and the whole team's outside it," Niekro said. "They had big rookies there, Silver Sluggers. I go up to the hotel and the manager says, 'Niekro, throw your luggage on the bus.' Standing out front with the team were Elrod Hendricks and Pat Jordan, who later became a well-known author.

"I set my luggage down and all of a sudden, Elrod Hendricks just drilled Pat Jordan. Punched him and knocked him down. I said, 'Damn! This is the west! We need to wear cowboy hats and spurs!'

"We were going to an Indian reservation to play some games. It took the bus seven, eight hours to get there, and we stayed for two or three days."

Niekro stuck with the team and went 7-2 as a reliever. The next year, he was back in minor-league spring training in Waycross. "Years later," Niekro said, "John Mullen [the Braves general manager from 1979-85] told me that during the organization meetings each spring, when a player's name came up and guys were asked for their opinion, only Birdie Tebbetts spoke up for me."

Tebbetts managed Cincinnati and Cleveland and, in between, the Braves at the end of the 1961 season and for all of '62. Each spring, he was Niekro's saving grace. In 1960, while Niekro was still struggling with the knuckler for control and effectiveness, he played Class-A ball with the Jacksonville, Florida, affiliate. His manager was Red Murff, who later became a scout for the Mets and signed a prospect who was the anti-Niekro: Nolan Ryan. In Jacksonville, though, Murff saw something in the skinny Ohio teenager with the wayward knuckleball.

"He told me, 'Niekro, if you can get the knuckleball over, you can pitch in the big leagues,'" recalled Niekro. "That rang a bell in my head. That was the deciding factor for me staying in the big leagues."

Niekro advanced to Double-A Austin, Triple-A Louisville, then spent a year in the military. In 1964, he finally became a starter with Triple-A Denver, starting 21 times, 13 of them complete games. Niekro was called up late that season and appeared 10 times out of the Braves bullpen. But he didn't become a part-time starter until 1967, then finally a full-time member of the rotation in '68.

And then came 1969.

"Probably my best season," said Niekro, who won 23 games and made the National League All-Star team for the first time. His 23rd victory came in the NL West Division clincher, when Niekro gave way to another knuckleballer of some note—Hoyt Wilhelm, who notched the save that day. In the inaugural National League Championship Series, Atlanta was swept 3-0 by the upstart, out-of-nowhere New York Mets. Their superb young pitching included not only Tom Seaver and Jerry Koosman, but a relatively unknown 22-year-old right-hander who came out of the bullpen in the third inning of Game 3 when Mets starter Gary Gentry was hurt, and who went the rest of the way to win the pennant: Nolan Ryan. Somewhere, Red Murff was smiling.

Atlanta was, too, despite the loss. "We were here three years, and then we won the [division] in 1969," Niekro said. "Nobody knew how the South would take to [major-league] baseball. I guess the fans

thought, 'We have something going here in the South with baseball.'"
Niekro paused. He smiled. "Little did they know. I remember in the
'70s, we averaged 6,000 a game, 7,000 a game."

From 1975-79, Atlanta won as many as 70 games just once. The
Braves were pitiful, the crowds so small that sometimes, during Fan
Appreciation Weekends late in the season, press box personnel and
out-of-town baseball writers would enter the stadium with their
credentials, then also buy the cheapest ticket available in hopes of
winning a prize. One year, a Dodgers beat writer won a dozen roses.
Yet year after year, loss after loss, Niekro soldiered on. How? "You've
got a choice," he said. "You can choose to let it bother you, or not to.
My philosophy has always been it's not where you've been, it's where
you're going. Who knows what's gonna happen in the next game?
You've got no control over the present. You've got no control over the
future. You've got control over right now.

"The losing? It's always tough, the losing," Niekro said. "If I knew
guys who weren't trying or were trying to lose, I'd be furious. But I
never believed in getting on guys' asses. I knew they were trying. Even
when I was a veteran, I wouldn't expect anybody to get on my ass if I
made a bad pitch.

"I remember one year when I was supposed to be the ace of the
staff and I started off 0-7, I got a letter from a lady in Chicago. She
watched the games on WTBS. There wasn't any cable or ESPN then.
She wrote, 'Mr. Niekro, I want you to think of these two things: You
can't always control what happens to you, but you can control how
you react to what happens to you. Number two, you're going to have
to learn to accept your losses without getting defeated.'

"I thought, 'How can I accept my ass getting beat?' But the more
I thought about it, it made sense," Niekro said. "If I lost, well, you
haven't [totally] defeated me yet. I still got the bat, got the glove, got
the ball. And I'll keep coming at you. You can knock me down, but
I'm getting up. And eventually, no matter how long it takes, I'm gonna
beat you.

"That was my thinking the rest of my career."

Niekro didn't know what to think one May day in 1977. The
Braves awoke that morning in Pittsburgh having lost 16 consecutive

games to the startling news that owner Ted Turner—who'd bought the team the previous year—had sent manager Dave Bristol away for a few days on a "scouting assignment." Turner was going to manage the team himself that evening. The scheduled Atlanta starting pitcher was Phil Niekro.

"We're at the ballpark, taking batting practice, and I'm getting my swings in the cage," he said. "There are reporters everywhere. And here comes Ted walking out of the clubhouse, in his uniform.

"You don't know what to think," Niekro said, still laughing three decades hence. "The only thing I knew was he was very successful in the America's Cup. He was a winner. But I didn't see any boats out there, or any sailors.

"He was spending money and getting his ass beat, and he wanted to know why. How much he knew about baseball, I didn't know. But I found out. Ted walked up to the batting cage and was watching me hit. I said, 'Ted, what spot you got me hitting in?'

"He said, 'Well, I don't know. Where you wanna hit? You wanna lead off? You wanna hit second?' I thought, 'Oh, I can just see me hitting ahead of Aaron.' So I said, 'Well, just keep me in my spot.' And we got beat again.

"Ted was a great guy. He'd come in with his shorts and Levis on, a little hat, and sit right next to the dugout. He'd have this chew [tobacco]. Every game, he'd come in and talk with the guys, whether we won or lost. He'd have a beer, or a chew, and talk with the guys—not just about baseball, about life. I never had an owner or a GM do that, except for Bill Lucas.

"I thought, 'What a great owner.' Good guy to be around," Niekro said of Turner. "Don't know how much he knew about baseball, but he was very interested in the players, their families. I really enjoyed playing for him."

When Bristol was fired at season's end, the five candidates to replace him as manager included one rather surprising name: Phil Niekro, who, at 39, also envisioned a throwback dual role for himself.

"I guess everybody who plays the game thinks they know about as much baseball as anybody else," he said. "They were looking for a manager. I knew the game and the players, so I threw my name in there. I had nothing to lose. I thought, 'I can be a playing manager, like Lou Boudreau [once a player-manager for Cleveland for nine seasons].'"

Instead, Atlanta opted for a relative unknown, with no previous major-league managing experience: Bobby Cox. By 1982, despite a winning season in his third year, Cox had been fired by Turner. The new manager was Joe Torre, the Braves' young slugging catcher in the late '60s and later the NL MVP with St. Louis before failing as manager of the Mets. Torre's second managerial go-round began spectacularly as the Braves posted a season-opening 13-game winning streak.

"I think the reason they won 13 games in a row is because I was on the DL," Niekro said, laughing. "I was a horrible Opening Day pitcher."

Two or three days before the season opener, which Niekro was scheduled to start, he was throwing batting practice (as was the custom then for starting pitchers, between starts). Braves pitcher Rick Mahler was hitting and asked, "One more pitch."

"I threw it and the ball looked like it was gonna be here," Niekro said, holding his hand just off the floor. "Mahler swung the bat like a golf club. Hit me right here." He held his left ribcage. "Bruised a rib. I told them I could still pitch, but they said no."

For Niekro, then 43, it was the first time he'd ever been placed on the disabled list. Once he finally got back on the mound, he never let up. He finished the '82 campaign 17-4, for a winning percentage of .810 that still stands as a club record. Niekro closed the season with consecutive complete-game shutouts at San Francisco and at San Diego to help hold off the Dodgers for the NL West title.

"Probably the two best back-to-back games I ever pitched, with what was at stake," he said. "And I hit a two-run homer in San Diego, too."

The Braves and Dodgers entered the final weekend tied for first place. On Friday, as Niekro prepared for his regular-season finale, "I remember all the San Diego players saying, 'We're gonna try and beat you guys. But we don't want the Dodgers to win,'" he said. That night, the Braves led 1-0, with Glenn Hubbard on second base, when Padres starter Eric Show threw Niekro a fat, belt-high fastball.

"I looked at Show," Niekro recalled, "and he. . ." Niekro said, grinning from ear to ear the way Show looked at him standing in the batter's box. "He had this funny look on his face. Now, I'm not saying anything, but. . . [the Padres] were out of [the race]. I thought, 'Why do you throw that ball right there?'

"Then I looked at his face, and it's, like [he was asking me], 'Why didn't you swing at that? Niekro, if you can't hit that one out of the ballpark. . . .' So I thought, 'He's gonna throw it again.' I lifted up my left leg this time, to get a little more power on [my swing], and there's the pitch again, and I hit it into the left-field stands for a two-run home run.

"I still, to this day, wonder why I didn't get one of Show's real good sliders? Maybe he was trying to fool me or something." Niekro smiled again.

In the opener of the '82 NLCS at Busch Stadium in St. Louis, Niekro took a 1-0 lead into the bottom of the fifth. There were two outs in the inning, just one out from making it an official game, which is relevant because it was raining hard. And this, after all, was a postseason game.

"I saw Billy Williams, the umpire, go over to [baseball commissioner] Bowie Kuhn, to talk," Niekro said. "I'm saying, 'C'mon, Billy, get back. I'll throw it over the middle [of the plate]. If he hits it out, he hits it out. They didn't want a playoff game decided in five innings. So they stopped play and waited. It rained and rained."

The game was rained out, and Major League Baseball decided to start Game 1 over from scratch. After St. Louis won the rescheduled opener 7-0, Niekro started Game 2. "I'm winning 3-2 after the sixth inning, and Torre pinch hits for me," he said. "Gene Garber comes in, and we lose 4-3.

"I was pitching well in St. Louis," he said. "I had 'em where I wanted them."

That would be Niekro's last shot at the postseason. After going 11-10 in '83, the guy everyone knew as "Knucksie," at age 44 and with 268 career victories, was released by the only organization he'd ever known.

"I was born a Brave, and I wanted to die a Brave," Niekro said. "I had my mind set on that. And that was the longest damn day I had in my life. The most depressed day in my life was that day."

Niekro signed a two-year contract with the Yankees, who were just starting to fall from grace. He won 16 games each season. After spending the '86 season in his native Ohio with the Indians, Niekro then nearly finished the '87 season—and his career—with a brief stint in Toronto.

"I had a month to go in '87, and I thought, 'I can't leave this game wearing a Toronto shirt,'" Niekro recalled. "So I went down to the Braves and worked out a deal with them to pitch one last game. Then I signed a contract for $1."

That September 27, for a team that would finish 69-92, Niekro returned for a proper, if quick, curtain call. He started against the Giants and worked three innings, then walked off the field for the final time as an Atlanta Brave.

"Then, that was it," Phil Niekro said. "Ten years later, the Hall comes."

GAME OF MY LIFE

"In 1985, I'm with the Yankees. My brother Joe is there, too. He'd just been traded from Houston to the Yankees. We were rooming together in a hotel in New Jersey, living in a suite.

"That summer, my father was very, very sick. And he's the guy who taught me the knuckleball. I come out and pitch in Yankee Stadium, and I win my 299th game. That's when I knew I could win 300 games. I had 299, and I had five more starts that season.

"After the game, Joe and I go back to the hotel in New Jersey. It's about 11:30, maybe midnight. The phone rings, and I pick it up. It's my mother, and she's crying. She said she was so upset she couldn't talk, so another lady takes over on the phone.

"She said, 'Phil, we're at the hospital, with your dad. The priest is here with your mom. He's given your dad last rites. You'd better get here.' I said, 'We can't get there 'til morning.'

"The next morning, Joe and I fly to Pittsburgh; then we drive to the hospital in Wheeling [West Virginia], which is about eight miles from Lansing, Ohio, our hometown. We get to the hospital, and there's Dad. He was about 6-foot-3, 220 pounds. But now he's lying in the bed, with needles and tubes in him everywhere. I can't even recognize him.

"Joe and I stay there four days. We didn't go home. We slept in the room. They brought in a cot, and a Lazy Boy. My dad hadn't said a word to us in the four days we were there. Now, it's time for me to pitch in New York.

"We're a half-game out of first. It's Saturday morning, and I've gotta make a decision. Joe and I need to fly back to New York. Dad's in the hospital, hasn't opened his eyes or said a word, and I've got to pitch. Neither Joe nor I know what to do. Joe looks at me and says, 'You know, I've heard when people are in this condition, they can hear you but can't talk.' I'd heard that too, but I said, 'Joe, he hasn't talked in four days or batted an eye. We've gotta make a decision.'

"Joe goes to the bed and leans over and says, 'I don't know if you can hear me, Dad, but we've gotta make a decision. If you can hear me, Dad, blink your eye.' And my dad blinked an eye. I said, 'Holy smokes, Joe! He's heard everything we've said for four days!

"Then my dad's right hand moved. Joe said, 'You think he wants to write something?' So Joe said, 'Dad, if you wanna write something, blink your eye.' My dad blinked again. I got a pad of paper, a hospital notepad, and put it by my dad's hand and laid a pencil on it. His lips started to move.

"Joe said, 'He's talking, Phil, he's talking!' Joe put his head down to listen but said, 'I don't know what he said. It was just warm air coming out of his mouth.' Then dad took the pencil, he was looking up, and his hand moved. Then he moved away the paper.

"I picked it up, and he'd written two words: W-I-N. H-A-P-P-Y. That told me what I've gotta do. I've gotta go to New York. I said, 'Okay, Dad, I'm going to New York to pitch a game and make you happy.' His hand went like this. [Niekro flicked his hand to the left]. It was like, 'Get your ass outta here and get to New York and pitch.'

"I took the paper with me, and I had it in the pocket of my uniform pants when I was walking to the bullpen with our pitching coach, Bill Monbouquette. But I lost the game. The next day, Joe and I fly back to Pittsburgh and drive to Wheeling. We stay three more days. Dad still hasn't said anything. So we fly to Milwaukee, and I lose again.

"This time, Joe stays on the road with the club. I fly back to Pittsburgh, drive to the hospital and stay with Dad four more days. Now, it's my third [crack at 300 wins]. I join the team in Baltimore this time. I've still got that paper in my pocket, but it's getting beat up and getting hard to read. I got beat *again*.

"Now I've got just two starts left in the season. My mom says, 'Why don't you stay with the team? It's not doing you any good coming back here. You're not getting your throwing [between starts] in.' So I do go, and I lose *again*.

"I've got one start left. It's the second and last year of my contract with the Yankees. I don't know if they're going to re-sign me. This was my last chance to win my 300th. That's what Dad's hanging around for.

"We go to Toronto. Bobby Cox is managing them, and we're three games behind with three games left in the season. We win Friday night, and we're down two. We lost Saturday, though, and Toronto clinches. Afterward, Joe and I stay up all night, talking about this game. We're having a few lemonades. We stay up all night; maybe we slept two hours. By this time, Dad's note is unreadable.

"Joe and I are talking, and I'm thinking, 'Will the Yankees re-sign me? Or maybe will the Braves take me back? I'm 46 years old. This is my last chance to win 300.'

"The next day, in the fifth inning, Willie Randolph, who's playing second base for us, comes in to the mound. He says, 'I'm getting all these signs from Butch'—Butch Wynegar was catching—'and giving them to the outfielders, and I haven't seen a knuckleball yet.' Well, I was making up pitches as I went along: eephus pitches, blooper pitches, I'm just making 'em up as I go along. Not one knuckleball.

"Come the ninth inning, we're up 9-0. And here I am, not knowing that Steinbrenner had hooked up a radio play-by-play of the game on the phone to my mother in the hospital, so she can give it to my dad.

"So, I win the game, my 300th win. Joe's the first one out to the mound to give me a hug. He says, 'Brother, I've gotta tell you something about Dad.' I'm expecting the worst. We sat in the dugout and Joe said, 'Dad woke up in the seventh inning and looked at Mom and said, 'Boy, he's pitching a helluva game.' I said, 'Joe, you're [kidding] me!'

"We fly to Pittsburgh the next day. Dad's out of intensive care. No more needles in him. He's sitting up. I put a Yankee hat on his head. I put that ball in his hand, and he's grinning from ear to ear.

"The doctor said, 'You guys had better get out of here. He's been up all night.' Dad went home and lived two more years. He saw one of his boys win 300 games. He saw both of his boys win 539 games, the most by any brothers in baseball history.

"Finally, when I was out of the game, and Joe was out of the game, he passed away. That was the greatest, most memorable game of my life. Dad got sick again, and Joe and I were there when he took his last breath. But the doctors couldn't explain why he didn't die earlier. He stuck around to see me win my 300th and Joe pitch in the '87 World Series with the Twins.

"But back to my 300th. I had not thrown a knuckleball the whole game. I had two outs in the ninth and two strikes on Jeff Burroughs, the old Brave. Butch Wynegar comes out to the mound and says, 'I know, you wanna throw a knuckleball.

"I said, 'I can't think of a better way to win 300 than with a knuckleball, what my dad taught me.' I look at Jeff, and he says, 'C'mon, pitch to me!'" Niekro paused, and grinned. "The only knuckleball I threw the whole ballgame. Jeff struck out and that's when Joe came running out of the dugout. I had my 300th."

Chapter 6

STEVE BEDROSIAN

You think "Braves," and naturally you think pitching. Exceptional pitching. Nonpareil pitching. You think Braves, and you think Cy Young winners. Or "Mound Rushmore," the nickname given by esteemed baseball scribe Marty Noble to the pitcher's mound at Turner Field.

You think Braves, and you think of Tom Glavine, the National League Cy Young Award winner in 1991, again in '98, and twice the runnerup. You think Braves, and you think of Greg Maddux, who arrived in Atlanta in 1993 as a high-priced free agent who'd just won his first Cy Young with the Cubs by edging out . . . Tom Glavine. And then Maddux won his second Cy Young with the Braves in '93, his third in '94 his fourth in '95. You think Braves, and you think of John Smoltz, who had the best stuff of anyone on those celebrated staffs of the '90s and early 21st century. Who went 24-8 in 1996, won four more games in the postseason that year, and easily captured the NL Cy Young that star-kissed season.

You think Braves, and you think Cy Young and you think . . . Steve Bedrosian? The guy known as Bedrock? Yes, Bedrosian, who as a rookie once helped the Braves win a long-awaited division title, but who had to leave Atlanta for Philadelphia before winning the rarest of Cy Youngs in 1987—as a reliever, on a fifth-place team.

You think that's a good pitching story? You don't know the half of it.

Let's start at the very beginning, a very good place to start tracking Bedrosian's big-league odyssey. Let's start in 1981, when a hard-throwing right-handed reliever was called up to Atlanta from Richmond after the mid-season strike. Bedrosian remembers it like it was yesterday. His recall, like many players, is remarkable in both scope and detail.

"I flew out to L.A. and met the team after the strike," Bedrosian said. "I came in for Gaylord Perry, and the bases were loaded with one out. I did good. I got a fly ball from [Ron] Roenicke and then struck out Rick Monday. And I got the win.

"But I was just hovering on that mound," he said. "Shaky as a green kid. Bobby was the manager then."

Bobby Cox was gone the next year, fired when Bedrosian and his 95 miles-per-hour fastball came up for good. He had a sensational year in '82 as a set-up man for new manager Joe Torre. Bedrosian appeared in 64 games, earned eight victories, had 11 saves. He also struck out 112 batters, the most by a reliever in the National League, and helped Atlanta win its first division title since 1969. Although Dodger Steve Sax edged him for NL Rookie of the Year honors, Bedrosian was named the National League's Rookie Pitcher of the Year by the *Sporting News*.

In 1983 and '84, working mostly as a set-up man for Gene Garber, but also as a closer when Garber was inconsistent, Bedrosian earned 19 and 11 saves respectively in those two years. But after moving into the rotation under new manager Eddie Haas and going just 7-15 as a starter (with no complete games in 37 starts), Bedrosian was traded—along with outfielder Milt Thompson—to Philadelphia for catcher Ozzie Virgil and Pete Smith.

"The first trade is always the shocker," said Bedrosian, who'd get accustomed to the process. "We were having dinner at [new closer] Bruce Sutter's that night. I got a call telling me that I'd been traded. The next message I got was from Bill Giles, welcoming me to the Phillies."

Bedrosian recalls the date precisely: December 6. "It was my birthday," said the pitcher, who'd turned 28 that day. The Bedrosians sold their home, rented for three years in Cherry Hill in South Jersey, and finally bought another house. Then, in June of '89, he was traded again—this time to San Francisco. "On Father's Day," said Bedrosian, the father of five children with his wife, Tammy. "It was a good move. We took over first place and went to the infamous Earthquake Series."

By then, Bedrosian had not only persevered, he'd triumphed in the most unexpected manner. He'd not only won over the notoriously critical Philly fans—at least initially—but also claimed a historic Cy Young Award.

"It was a tough crowd [in Philadelphia]," Bedrosian recalled. "Ozzie [Virgil] was an All-Star. I had struggled." By early '89, "The crowd was getting on me. Tough fans. Hey, it took [Hall of Fame third baseman Mike] Schmidt 13 years [to win fan approval]."

Not so in '87, however. After a solid debut in 1986 (an 8-6 record, with 29 saves in 68 games), Bedrosian got off to an awful start the following season. "I started out 1-3, with an 8.91 ERA," he recalled. "When the weather started warming up, I warmed up.

"I remember just getting in position and grabbing the ball," Bedrosian said. "Lee Elia was the manager. I think John Felske got fired. In Philly, they gave me a chance. They said take the ball and run with it."

Bedrosian took the suggestion to heart. In 65 appearances, he earned a league-high 40 saves, with a 5-3 record and earned-run average of 2.83.

"I remember it was bittersweet," he said of that season. "We hadn't won as a team. I had a great year. Kent Tekulve did a great job of setting me up, going the seventh inning, or seventh and eighth and putting the ball in my hands."

The significance of his accomplishment wasn't lost on Bedrosian. "I knew there had only been a handful [of relievers] who'd preceded me," said Bedrosian, who became just the sixth relief pitcher to win a Cy Young. "I was blessed." It helped that no starting pitcher had set the NL ablaze.

"[Rick] Sutcliffe, [Rick] Reuschel, they each had 17, 18 wins apiece," Bedrosian said. "I just kept saving games, and people said, 'Hey, you've got a chance.' I didn't get caught up in it.

"I don't want to say I backed into it," he said. "But the numbers, well, that's what the [BBWAA] writers thought, and how they voted. The voting was close, probably the closest ever."

Bedrosian won with 57 points. Sutcliffe finished second with 55, Reuschel third with 54.

"It [winning as a closer] meant a lot," he said. "I was thankful for the opportunities, and to be in position to get there. I got to go [up to New York] on *Good Morning America* with the famous Roger Clemens. That was his first Cy Young. Being from Massachusetts, I got to rub elbows with him. Growing up, Yaz [Red Sox Hall of Famer Carl Yastrzemski, the last man to win the Triple Crown, in 1977] wasn't my favorite. I liked Rico Petrocelli, and Jim Lonborg."

He also liked a sense of stability and security, two quality-of-life issues that are often missing for ballplayers. They were for Bedrosian, even in the best of times. Consider the family's sheepdog, nicknamed "Rumor." Full name: "Bedrock's Trade Rumor." Rumors were rampant.

"I'd been rumored to be going to San Francisco, Kansas City, other places," Bedrosian said. "It came down in the seventh inning in the bullpen. I was going to San Francisco. On Father's Day."

The Bedrosians bought a house in Foster City, California, about a half-hour south of Candlestick Park, down near San Mateo. Bedrosian (who'd saved 103 games in his three-plus seasons in Philadelphia) made 40 appearances for San Francisco, got 17 saves and helped get the Giants back into the World Series for the first time since 1962. There, they ran into Oakland's "Bash Brothers" of Mark McGwire and Jose Canseco, and also into a far more powerful force: Mother Nature.

"We were about to start Game 3," Bedrosian said. "I think the Gatlin Brothers were about to sing the national anthem. I was standing on the top step of the dugout." That's when the earthquake hit.

"I started getting a little queasy," he said. "Being from Massachusetts, we're not used to them. The fans were cheering. They knew what happened. Then the [news] reports started coming in. I remember them letting the players and their families go home first. What was normally a 30-minute ride home to Foster City became a four-hour ride.

"My mom didn't feel good that day," Bedrosian remembered. "She didn't go to the game. She stayed down at our house in Foster City. She likes to play video games, and was playing a video game, sitting on the floor, when my dog started scratching at the door. He had a sixth sense.

"My mom got up to let him in," he said, "and the TV where she had been sitting fell over where she was. She was OK, but I remember we waited about 10 days before playing again."

The A's swept away the Giants in four games. After playing a full season in San Francisco the following year, Bedrosian found himself in the American League, pitching for the Minnesota Twins. Come October, he was bound for the World Series again. This time against his original club, the Braves.

"That was a lot of fun. I had a lot of friends on the Braves," said Bedrosian, who appeared in three Series games against his ex-teammates and pals—all in Atlanta-Fulton County Stadium. The first two were tight, dramatic, one-run Atlanta victories. In Game 5, Bedrosian worked a mop-up inning in the Braves' resounding 14-5 rout. But it was Bedrosian who finally earned a World Series championship ring, the Twins triumphant after a pair of thrilling one-run, extra-inning victories. "It could have gone either way," said Bedrosian, who was 5-3 in 56 appearances that season, with six saves. "It was just a great World Series."

It also appeared to be the end for Bedrock. In June of '91, a startling trend began: Bedrosian would awake in the morning of a hot summer day, only to find the index and middle fingers on his right—or pitching—hand felt as frozen as a Minnesota winter. Ever thorough, Bedrosian began seeking medical answers, undergoing tests, nerve exams, ultrasound treatment, and acupuncture. He saw a chiropractor. Carpal tunnel syndrome was ruled out. Bedrosian wondered if his old habit of chewing tobacco was the culprit. Perhaps the nicotine had contaminated the blood vessels in those fingers? No. Doctors discounted stress, or trauma from a hard-hit grounder off his pitching hand.

"I really thought I was done," Bedrosian said. "Just out of the game for good."

He sat out all of the 1992 season. Then suddenly and mysteriously the numbness subsided and the feeling returned to his two fingers. Still living on a 120-acre family farm in Senoia, Georgia, near Newnan, Bedrosian contacted the Braves that winter. He understood the club's concerns; his velocity had dipped dramatically in '91. With good reason: "I only had three fingers."

The Braves welcomed Bedrosian back to spring training with no guarantees, merely as a non-roster invitee. Bobby Cox, back managing since midway through the 1990 season, felt Bedrosian might still be able to pitch. He knew about his professionalism, work ethic, and Cy Young resume.

"There were four guys competing for three positions: Mark Davis, Jay Howell, Greg McMichael, and me," Bedrosian said. "Mark Davis was the guy who didn't make it. I got three more beautiful years in."

After a slow start that spring, Bedrosian pitched well enough to earn a spot in Atlanta's bullpen. The regular season started slowly, too, with two defeats in April—one on a first-pitch, 11th-inning home run by former Giants teammate Matt Williams. At one point, Bedrosian didn't pitch for 16 straight days. He had to earn Cox's trust again, which he eventually did. "This is all gravy now," Bedrosian said that July, en route to finishing 5-2 that season with a career-low 1.63 ERA. In the strike-shortened '94 season, he was 0-2 in 46 appearances but struck out 43 batters in 46 innings.

While the Braves finally, blessedly won the World Series in 1995—Bedrosian made 29 appearances that year, but his effectiveness was clearly gone—Bedrock's true championship season was 1994. That was "Cody's season"—specifically the night of May 10.

GAME OF MY LIFE

"It was a tribute to Cody," Bedrosian now recalls.

Cody, Tammy and Steve's second son, was three years old when his father was pitching for the Giants in 1990. That year, Cody fell ill during spring training. For several months, actually. Initially, doctors thought the young boy might have rheumatoid, or childhood, arthritis. A bone marrow biopsy showed otherwise: leukemia. Bedrosian recalled the diagnosis as if "someone put a gun to your head."

The Giants opened that season in Atlanta. Bedrosian remembers a phone call from Tammy in California: "You need to get out here." He did, and they received the kind of diagnosis every parent dreads. "We just looked at each other and said, 'God, we're going to make it better, do what we have to do and fight the fight.' And that's what we did."

The Bedrosians immediately checked Cody into a hospital that evening. Steve spent the next 10 days with his son. To hell with pitching. He finally returned to Candlestick the night the Giants were presented their '89 National League championship rings before their home opener. Giants manager Roger Craig asked Bedrosian if he could pitch.

"I said, 'Sure,'" he said. "I hadn't pitched in 15 days." Bedrosian came on in the ninth inning and surrendered a game-winning homer to Benito Santiago.

"It was really tough then," Bedrosian now says. He watched his young son endure chemotherapy, medication, shots, spinal taps. Cody's illness, he said, "Made you stronger as a person, and made us stronger as a family. Cancer can make you closer or tear you apart."

Cody's leukemia went into remission. But as Bedrosian said prophetically in the summer of '93, "It can come back at anytime." The leukemia returned, aggressively, several months later. Cody underwent more extensive, painful treatment, including a bone marrow transplant. In his illness, the boy was as resolute as his father had always been on the mound.

Fast forward to May, 1994. The night of tribute to Cody, who was six by then and very sick. That evening, some two dozen Bedrosian family members, relatives, and friends were sitting in section 101 in Atlanta-Fulton County Stadium. They all stood and cheered when Cody and his older brother, Kyle, walked to the mound to throw out the first pitch.

Cody went first, throwing to his father. The crowd roared as Cody doffed his Braves cap and beamed. When Kyle perfectly mimicked his younger brother, the crowd roared anew. Bedrosian signed the balls for his boys, and then father and sons posed for a photo.

"It's funny," Bedrosian says now. "I thought everything was going to go great that night. I was going to get in the game and do great. I didn't. I got shelled."

To honor Cody and his father, several Braves wore their game pants knee-high that night, as Bedrosian always did. Some also wore their sock stirrups high, in Bedrock fashion. Despite that, the game started slowly for the Braves, then seemingly disintegrated for the Bedrosian family in the seventh inning, when Steve relieved Mark Wohlers.

"Incaviglia crushed it," Bedrosian recalled. Philadelphia's Pete Incaviglia launched a tape-measure grand slam that Bedrosian never even turned his head to track. He knew. The ball traveled 481 feet, landing in the club level and deflating the Bedrosian clan in the stands. That made it 8-1 Phillies, and in section 101, Kyle Bedrosian could only hold his left hand to his head in despair.

In the bottom of the ninth, the outcome surely certain, Cody and his grandfather stood and headed up the aisle. Cody suddenly ran back down to retrieve the ball he'd thrown out before the game. Then grandfather and grandson walked up the aisle and made their way down into the Braves clubhouse to see Steve. Instead, the saw a miracle occur on TV.

"I'd felt so dejected," Bedrosian said. "I felt like I'd let Cody down, my teammates down. But my teammates picked me up. It was almost like it was a storybook ending."

From the downer of Bedrock, there's a page right out of history. The bottom of the ninth proved seventh heavenly. Literally. The

Braves rapped single after single after single. Mike Mordecai belted his first big-league home run. Javy Lopez drove in the tying run. Miraculously, the Braves had tied the score, 8-8. Bedrosian was off the hook, yet the game was far from over.

Cody and his grandfather watched on the clubhouse television through the 10th inning. And 11th. And 12th, 13th, and 14th. Finally, with two out in the bottom of the 15th, Braves reliever Mike Stanton bunted home Deion Sanders with the winning run.

"It *was* a storybook ending," Bedrosian said. "Who would've thought it would've ended that way?"

It ended with Steve and Cody standing in the clubhouse as the delirious Braves made their giddy way up the tunnel from the dugout. "I stood in the locker," Bedrosian said, "and watched everyone congratulate and hug Cody."

"Before it even started, this game was for Cody," Stanton said that night. "Having him in here, going through what he's gone through, a comeback victory like that makes this victory even more special for him.

"You look what he's gone through, you notice baseball isn't important," he continued. "You see all the fight in his eyes and all the love in Steve's eyes, and baseball isn't important. If baseball gives Cody happiness, it probably means more than anything tonight."

Bedrosian fondly recalls the attention his teammates gave his son. "Deion Sanders was the biggest person who befriended Cody and took him under his wing," Bedrosian said. "Deion, and Mike Stanton. A lot of people look at Deion in a different way. But if you get to know him, he's a great guy.

"I don't know if it's because he played two sports or rubbed people the wrong way," he said. "But he made Cody sparkle. And we got through it with teammates like Deion. Stanton. [John] Smoltz and Brett Butler."

Best of all, Cody got healthy once again. His leukemia was cured, and he went on to play some baseball himself. At least for a few years.

"He hung up his spikes at 12," Bedrosian said. "He said, 'Dad, I really don't want to play anymore.' I said, 'That's fine with me.'"

Cody's now a student at the Art Institute of Atlanta in suburban Dunwoody. He's interested in cinematography and thinking of a career in movie-making. That's fine with his father, too.

Of his son's, and his family's, fight against leukemia, Steve Bedrosian now says he's happy to share his experience with others. "When other people's kids get sick, they call us. Or our preacher calls us and we talk to them. To help them get through it."

Much as his teammates did for him on a night where all hope looked lost.

Chapter 7

LEO MAZZONE

The Pope of Pitching.

That's what Roger Kahn anointed Leo Mazzone. In his 2000 book The Head Game—Baseball Seen From the Pitcher's Mound, Kahn, the celebrated baseball writer and author of The Boys of Summer, entitled the final chapter, "The Pope of Pitching."

All about Pope Leo I.

Imagine that: Rockin' Leo, the little Atlanta Braves pitching coach from the summer of 1990 through the 2005 season, elevated to the high priest of pitching, baseball's finest art.

"One of my greatest compliments ever," Mazzone said. "To be in the same company with the other people in that book, is one of the greatest compliments I could ever receive."

From 1992-2002, the Braves' pitching staff finished first or second in earned-run average in the major leagues. "It's the greatest pitching run in the history of the game," Mazzone said. "There's no question about it."

In the last year of that 11-season span of pitching excellence, Atlanta led the majors with a 3.13 staff earned-run average in 2002,

69

the lowest for the team since a 3.05 ERA in 1974. The Braves also had a major league-low bullpen ERA of 2.60 in '02. That season, John Smoltz, the one-time 24-victory Cy Young Award winner-turned-closer, set a National League record with 55 saves on a surgically repaired right elbow. Chris Hammond, the left-handed reliever who was out of baseball in 2000 and '01, was virtually untouchable under Mazzone; his ERA of 0.95 was just the third sub-1.00 ERA (minimum 70 innings pitched) compiled since 1900.

All that (and another NL East Division title) under the tutelage of Mazzone, the little bald guy who was always perched beside manager Bobby Cox in the Braves dugout, nervously rocking from the waist, from anxiety and excitement, forward and back. In good times and in bad, for better or worse, Leo Mazzone rocks. So, invariably, did his pitchers.

"Coaches get a lot better when you have Tom Glavine, Smoltzie, Steve Avery, and Charlie Leibrandt," Mazzone said, recalling Atlanta's magical worst-to-first 1991 season and that starting rotation in his first full season as the Braves pitching coach. "And you add Mad Dog [Greg Maddux] to the equation a few years later, and I'm really smart.

"It was all coming together in September of '90, when nobody really noticed," said Mazzone. "But we had four guys—Glav, Smoltzie, Ave, and Leibrandt—pitching pretty good. By the middle of '91, when we went into New York and swept the Mets, Bobby said to me, 'Leo, I think your young guys are growing up.' But it was coming together in September of '90.

"With those guys right there, you had the base for the old-fashioned, old-time great rotations—if they stayed healthy and went to the post," Mazzone said. "Our theme was, 'Go to the post when it's your turn.'"

By then, Mazzone had adopted the pitching philosophy of the great Johnny Sain, the former Boston Braves starter who became a pitching guru.

"Johnny came up in a four-man rotation," said Mazzone, who never advanced beyond Class AA ball (with Amarillo in the Texas League) as a left-handed pitcher, but fell under Sain's spell while working his way up in the Braves organization. "He pitched one side

session in between starts and started every fourth day. With today's five-men rotations, the [conventional] thinking was you [still] threw only once between starts.

"But my thought process was you stay stronger in a four-man, so I had my five-man rotations throw twice between starts," said Mazzone. "The whole thing is you throw more often with less exertion. That's the key. Our goal has always been for our pitchers not to miss any starts."

The epitome of that approach? In 1993 (when Maddux arrived in Atlanta and won the second of his unprecedented four consecutive Cy Young Awards), each of Atlanta's top four starters—Maddux, Glavine, Smoltz, and Avery—made 35 or more starts and worked at least 220 innings.

"In '93, we were trying to catch the Giants but we were way out in July," said Mazzone. "But Avery told me, 'We have 'em now, Leo.' I said, 'Ave, I'm glad you feel that way, but we're 7½ out.' He said, '[John] Burkett and [Bill] Swift [of the Giants] said they were starting to get tired after throwing over 150 innings. We got 'em, Leo, 'cause we don't kick in until after 150.'

"It was the mind-set of all those guys," Mazzone said. "They didn't want to miss starts. We preached, 'Come back a day early. Think complete game.' It all goes back to Johnny Sain, and you have to have a manager who makes pitching his priority. And Bobby made pitching his priority."

And Leo never complicated things. As Mazzone told Kahn, "Why turn something as simple as throwing into a science project?" Braves pitchers followed Mazzone's direction; he, in turn, followed Sain's tenets: "Pitch off your fastball, down and away," Mazzone said. "A fastball with movement. And change speeds. Very simple. If you do that, you're gonna win. If you can't, it's 50-50.

"You've gotta practice it," he said. "Get on the mound and, with proper mechanics, take a direct shot at the down-and-away strike, and change speeds.

"But," Rockin' Leo said, smiling, "you have to have talent."

Indeed, Mazzone knows there are skeptics and critics who claim his pitching staff's success was due solely to the talent of Maddux,

Glavine, Smoltz, Avery, Denny Neagle, the young Kevin Millwood, Russ Ortiz, and Mike Hampton.

"There's always gonna be some [jerks] who'll say, 'The only reason Mazzone does what he does is because of who he has,'" he said. "There's no question, I ain't stupid enough to know that there's gotta be great talent in order to do what we did all those years in that stretch. I mean, I ain't that stupid. But the other people, they can keep their mouths shut."

The Pope of Pitching? He'll keep talking. Writing, too. Mazzone is the co-author of two books: *Pitch Like A Pro*, with Jim Rosenthal; and *Leo Mazzone's Tales from the Braves Mound*, with Scott Freeman. He also released an instructional video, *Four Aces*.

"I could never be more satisfied in my professional career," Mazzone said. "I've realized all my dreams through these pitchers. I've realized what greatness is all about. The World Series, the playoffs, I never thought I'd get there.

"I have a tape library of all these great games we've had: Avery in Game 6 of the '91 NLCS in Pittsburgh; Smoltzie in Game 7 of the '91 World Series; Mad Dog winning Game 1 of the '95 World Series; Glav winning Game 6 1-0 to win it."

All that changed, however, after the 2005 season. Mazzone, who'd once flirted with becoming the New York Yankees pitching coach, finally left Atlanta to work for the Baltimore Orioles and manager Sam Perlozzo, his longtime boyhood friend. Mazzone received a significant bump in pay and a jarring jolt of reality. Even before the season began and his new staff eventually struggled through a tough season, Mazzone found the transition initially difficult, too.

"When I went to spring training in Fort Lauderdale, it was very awkward for the first few days," Mazzone said. "And when we opened up the season in Baltimore, not Atlanta, it was very awkward, too. When you spend 15 years with Bobby Cox and then you're not there with him anymore, it's tough.

"But when you see how powerful the American League was, it's unbelievable," he said. "They beat the hell out of the National League in inter-league play.

"But the Braves teams we had, we would've taken on any American League teams I saw this year, and I feel confident we would've won," Mazzone said. "You're talking about three Hall of Fame pitchers. They had that kind of ability, and that mind-set. It's a different ballgame."

A very different ballgame, indeed, for the Pope of Pitching.

"We had 11 pitchers with 20 or more saves in Atlanta," said Mazzone. "Eighteen 18-game winners; nine 20-game winners; Six Cy Youngs. One more World Series win would've solidified the damn thing. But we apologized to no one for our track record."

GAME OF MY LIFE

"Because of the personal feelings I had about Yankee Stadium, the game of my life would have to be the first game of the 1996 World Series.

"We'd already played the World Series in Minnesota and Toronto. We won it in '95 against Cleveland. But to me, because of my feelings about the Yankees, the first game in Yankee Stadium is the greatest moment of my career.

"I felt all my boyhood dreams about baseball had finally come true. My idol was always Whitey Ford. There was Mickey Mantle. It was just the entire setting. I saw Whitey each year in spring training. Whitey, Yogi Berra. Catfish Hunter, before he passed away, Tony Kubek, Clete Boyer. And I did have a chance to meet Mickey Mantle and Roger Maris. That night, for Game 1, Joe DiMaggio threw out the first pitch.

"The day before, during the workout, I stood on the mound. Then I went out and stood in center field, where DiMaggio and Mantle played. I went to see all the monuments. I took it all in. I got goose bumps. Whatever hair I still had stood up.

"It was a very emotional time for me, the first day. The first two days, actually: The workout day and the first game. Smoltzie was starting. And oh, what they do in Yankee Stadium, on that big screen: all the footage of Ruth, Gehrig, DiMaggio, Mantle, Whitey. Whitey was a 5-foot-9 left-hander who I thought had the greatest nickname of all time: the Chairman of the Board. And I was built the same way, too. That's where the similarities between us ended!

"As many Yankee fans as there were, as many people hated the Yankees as loved them. It got to be like that with us, too. I always took it as a compliment with the Braves when people said they were sick of seeing us in the World Series, like people had been with the Yankees. It made you feel good. When you walked into Yankee Stadium with Maddux and Glavine and Smoltz, you felt even better.

"You know, I don't think I ever was in Yankee Stadium before then. No, I'd never been in Yankee Stadium until then. Dad would take me to the old ballpark in Baltimore to see the Orioles. He'd take me to Griffith Stadium in D.C. to see the Senators. We'd go up to Pittsburgh sometimes and see the Pirates. But I'd never been to Yankee Stadium, the cathedral of baseball.

"From the moment you pulled up to the stadium, in the bus, and looked up and saw the stadium, you realized where you were. Then walking up and into the stadium. And then walking inside, downstairs in the tunnel, and you're walking where the greatest players who ever played had walked.

"Game 1 was when Andruw hit the two homers and Smoltzie shut 'em down. Then Mad Dog shut 'em out in Game 2. I think that's the greatest team we ever had, the '96 team. Well, '95—when we won it all—and '96. When we won the pennant in '91 and '92, we were very young. In '95 and '96, we were a major powerhouse. In '97, too. By '99, we weren't as good as the Yankees."

Chapter 8

RON GANT

There have been other bike rides of note. Mary Poppins, for instance. E.T., in that kid's bicycle basket, escaping up, up, and away into the sky, silhouetted against the moon. And Lance Armstrong, of course, any time he pedaled up the Alps and then sipped champagne while cycling triumphantly down the Champs d'Elyssee.

Yet in the long history of baseball, no one has ever had a more memorable, and costly, bike ride than Ron Gant. Or as *The New Biographical History of Baseball*, in chronicling the consequences of that multimillion-dollar mishap on February 3, 1994, describes it, "Gant incurred the most expensive broken leg in baseball history." Indeed, in a matter of moments, Gant lost more than $4 million and went from being a one-time MVP candidate to an ATV casualty. More immediately, it ended his Braves career, one that had had some spectacular peaks if a few confounding valleys, too.

"Who knows what might have happened?" Gant asks now. Who, indeed? On that wintry February day in '94, Gant went out for a bike ride with a few of his regular riding buddies. It wasn't a street bike, he said. No, not a typical motorcycle at all. "It was a dirt bike." An off-road, all-terrain bike, one that Gant loved to ride. They were riding in an area about 45 minutes north of Atlanta, an area that's now called Bridgemill. "Near where I live now," Gant said. "About five minutes away."

There was much to celebrate, and to look forward to. Spring training was a couple of weeks away, and the Braves—who'd won the National League pennant in 1991 and '92—were coming off a third consecutive NL West Division title. Gant had supplied much of Atlanta's right-handed power during that run, and he'd been rewarded with a one-year, $5.5 million contract.

It was, at the time, the largest one-year deal in history and made him the club's highest-paid player. He was also an experienced dirt biker. But, he recalled, "It was pretty wet that day. It had rained for a few days. We were jumping, and I slipped and broke my leg." His right leg was broken in two places, and Gant faced a long, uncertain recovery period. There was no guarantee that he'd make a complete comeback. So the Braves made a difficult, but financially practical, decision: They released Gant on March 15 and paid him $901,000— 30 days of termination pay. If the Braves had waited another day, they would have been obligated to pay Gant's full salary whether he played that season or not. Also, he was due to become a free agent at that season's end.

Eventually, Gant did sign a free agent contract with Cincinnati after sitting out that year, had considerable success, and went on to play until Oakland released him a month into the 2003 season. But those heady, if erratic, early years in Atlanta and then the halcyon days of 1991-93—when Gant averaged 28 home runs, 101 RBIs, and 31 stolen bases a season—were over.

A shame, really.

"The way I look at it is, before the accident happened, the Braves said they wouldn't sign any of their young players to multiyear deals," said Gant, who now does broadcasting in Atlanta for Fox Sports Net, including commentary on some Braves telecasts. "A few weeks later, they signed Jeff Blauser to a multiyear deal, and then David Justice.

"To me, signed for one year, my thinking went, 'They didn't want me,'" Gant said. "They were saying, 'We like you, but we don't like

you that much.' So who knows what would've happened? There were some other teams interested in signing me, including Boston."

Surely Gant, with his right-handed, pull-hitting power would've been a fine fit in Fenway Park, with the Green Monster just a short swat away in left field. He'll never know. We'll never know. This much is certain: In the first half of his major-league career, Ron Gant had some memorable moments and put up some remarkable numbers. Especially for a guy who was just 6 feet tall and weighed 200 pounds. But Gant was a devoted bodybuilder. And early on, he built a body of baseball work that was, at times, eye-popping. His was a rare combination of power and speed.

Gant came up as an infielder late in the 1987 season and hit the first of his 206 career home runs off a future Hall of Famer: Nolan Ryan. Called up from Triple-A Richmond early in the '88 season, Gant was the Braves' regular second baseman. He led all big-league rookies in most of the significant offensive categories: homers (19), RBIs (60), runs scored (85), extra-base hits (55), and triples (eight).

Early on, both his speed and power were evident, if not his infield expertise. "That's why when the whole Alfonso Soriano thing was going on, I wanted to call and tell him, 'Go to the outfield,'" said Gant, who, long before Soriano, moved from second base and found a home playing in the outfield. "And he took off. If I'm the [Washington] Nationals organization, I'd definitely want to keep him in the outfield, with the numbers he put up."

Unlike Soriano, Gant was never a 40-40-40 player: 40 homers, 40 steals, 40 doubles. But Gant had several 30-30 seasons that were very noteworthy in his era. Not before, however, going through some literal ups and downs. In 1989, Gant was shifted to third base. While adjusting to a new position, his batting average virtually flat-lined. He batted just .172 in the first 60 games, while committing 16 errors. Was this the same kid who'd finished fourth in the NL Rookie of the Year voting? Gant wasn't just demoted; he was sent all the way down to Class-A Sumter, South Carolina. His instructions were two-fold: rediscover your batting stroke, and learn how to play the outfield.

"I didn't want to go back down to the minors," Gant recalled. "But I knew it would be best for me to learn how to play the outfield. When I came back in 1990, I was a madman."

He was also Atlanta's new starting center fielder and, in the opinions of *Sports Illustrated* and *USA Today*, the National League's Comeback Player of the Year. Gant became just the 13th 30-30 player in major-league history, hitting 32 home runs and stealing 33 bases. He also batted a career-high .303. He'd repeat the 30-30 feat the following season, too, then have his greatest season in '93. In hindsight, however, Gant says of his 30-30 heroics and run production, "It seemed like it wasn't enough for them to want to keep me."

In 1991, Gant again smacked 32 homers and stole 34 bases, joining Willie Mays and Bobby Bonds as the only players—up to that time—to record consecutive 30-30 seasons. Gant had big hits, too. Significant hits. He led the majors with 21 game-winning hits that year, many of which helped fuel the Braves' miraculous worst-to-first pennant push. Gant finished sixth in the NL Most Valuable Player balloting and won a Silver Slugger award as one of the league's three best offensive outfielders. In a riveting NL Championship Series versus Pittsburgh, he set an NLCS record with seven steals.

He saved the most eye-popping moment of the season, though, for the World Series against Minnesota. With Lonnie Smith on first base, Gant singled in the third inning of Game 2 at the Metrodome. "[Smith] went to third and I rounded first base pretty hard," he recalled. "It's the World Series. I was going hard. The ball comes back in the infield. The Twins see me rounding the base hard and they throw to first, but I get back in time."

Just in time to get to know Kent Hrbek better. The Twins' first baseman was a big World Wrestling Federation aficionado. He then demonstrated what he'd learned from watching all those WWF telecasts. "The hefty tag," one sportswriter called it.

"When I hit the bag, Hrbek caught the ball and hooked my right leg with his glove and kind of pulled my leg off the bag," Gant said. "The umpire called me out, and I went ballistic. I remember being so mad, I threw my helmet toward the umpire. I don't know how they didn't throw me out of the game, but I think they knew I was right."

The umpire's call stood. It was a crucial out in what would become a 3-2 Twins win when Scott Leius hit a leadoff homer off Tom Glavine in the eighth inning. Ultimately, Minnesota would prevail in seven games, winning all four at home. Perhaps that wasn't accidental.

"Do you know that two off-seasons ago, the guy who ran the air-conditioning system in the Metrodome admitted he manipulated the system?" Gant said. Indeed, the man confessed to turning on the system so the air was blowing out toward the outfield whenever the Twins batted. It was off, and deadly still, when Atlanta was at bat.

"We suspected it," Gant said. "Even Bobby Cox said, 'Ron hit a ball so hard. . . .' It was the ball Kirby Puckett jumped up and caught against the Plexiglass in left field. They show [the highlight] all the time."

That was in the top of the 12th inning of Game 6. Puckett then led off the bottom half with a home run off Charlie Leibrandt that evened the Series at three games apiece. "Bobby said, 'That's one of the hardest-hit balls I've ever seen,'" Gant said. "What do I think of when I see that highlight? I think about the air-conditioning guy."

Gant also thinks about the miracle of '91, an unexpected treasure that helped transform a team and its city. "It was a lot of fun to be part of," he said. "A lot of people say it's the best World Series ever, or if not the top one, then in the top 1-2-3. From '91 to '93, the part that means the most, of course, is winning.

"When I came up in '88, and in '89 and '90, we were the worst," Gant said. "No one was concerned about the Braves. No one came to the games. [We were] the laughingstock of baseball. But that all changed."

Never more so than on the night of October 14, 1992—Game 7 of the NLCS, when Frankie swung and Sid slid. The Pittsburgh Pirates, who'd lost the '91 NLCS in seven nerve-wracking games against Atlanta, carried a 2-0 lead into the ninth inning of Game 7 in '92. In one of the greatest rallies in baseball history, the heroes ultimately would be Braves teammates Francisco Cabrera and Sid Bream.

"I was two hitters ahead of Cabrera," recalled Gant, who'd suffered through a horrible slump the second half of the season, including a 30-game drought in which he didn't hit a homer. "And I hit a ball and just missed it. I just missed hitting a home run; [Barry] Bonds went up against the [left-field] wall and made the catch. But I still drove in a run with a sacrifice fly. . . . Then I was up on the steps of the dugout, just cheering: 'C'mon, Francisco, get a hit!' I knew he was going to do it. He'd been doing it all year."

Still, Cabrera was called on to pinch hit with two out and two runners in scoring position. "I'd never been through a game with that much intensity and that much at stake," Gant said, "where we were down and thinking we were going to lose. And to go from that to the ultimate high. To the World Series."

Cabrera singled to left and David Justice, who'd reached on an uncharacteristic error by Jose Lind, scored easily from third. But then Sid Bream had to beat Barry Bonds' throw home. He did, barely. Pennant pandemonium ensued.

"The whole stadium was euphoric," Gant said. "I remember diving on the pile." The pile of players at home plate. Oh, the humanity piled atop Bream. "Getting up off of Sid and the pile," said Gant, "I looked up in the stands and the ushers and security guards were jumping up and down, some of them on top of the dugout. It was so loud in there, you couldn't hear."

Gant, however, hit just .182 in that NLCS and Cox sat him for most of the World Series against Toronto, which beat the Braves in six games. In 1993, Gant was transcendent, rebounding with career highs in homers (36) and RBIs (117). Half his home runs either gave Atlanta the lead or a win. In the furious race to catch San Francisco, Gant had 25 RBIs in his last 20 games.

"The way we looked at it was, every game was a playoff for the last month, month and a half of the season," Gant said. "We had to catch the Giants. By the time we got to the playoffs and played the Phillies, we were just mentally exhausted. We looked like we were out of gas."

Gant was out of luck just over three months later after his accident. Come 1995, he was a Cincinnati Red and an NL All-Star for the second time, finishing with 29 homers, 88 RBIs, and a .276 average. "Guess who beat us to go to the World Series," Gant said, laughing and recalling Atlanta's four-game sweep en route to the Series and its first world championship. That winter, Gant signed a free-agent contract with St. Louis and spent three seasons with the

Cardinals. In the '96 NLCS, Gant hit two homers off Tom Glavine in Game 1 and the Cards took a three games-to-one lead.

"And we lost to the Braves again," he chuckled, speaking of the Braves' comeback win in the '96 NLCS. "It was tough. I had a lot of incentive. Most guys that get traded, or something goes wrong with the organization they came up with, they're going to have that [incentive] enter sometime."

In 1998, Gant was an eyewitness to history. Home run history, courtesy of Mark McGwire. "I was two hitters after McGwire that night," Gant said of the evening of September 8, 1998, when McGwire broke Roger Maris' record of 61 home runs by lining his 62nd over the left-field wall in St. Louis. It was the culmination of a season, and a chase, the likes of which baseball had never seen. "To see what Mark was doing was unbelievable," said Gant. "Wherever we went, thousands and thousands of fans would show up to see him. They'd show up early to see him take [batting practice]. As a player, I'd never seen a guy hit the ball that hard. It was incredible."

"I know how hard it is to do that, to hit home runs," said Gant. "And he was making it look like child's play that season. It was mind-boggling to see how zoned in he was all year. And I'm not just talking about first-level homers. I'm talking about mezzanine, upper-deck shots.

"And with Sammy Sosa chasing McGwire, well, those two guys—all year long—were just changing the history of the game. It was so much fun to be a part of."

It was much less enjoyable to be traded to Philadelphia after that season in a multiplayer deal. Gant spent a year and a half in that city; it only seemed so much longer.

"Philly's a tough place to play," he said. "If you're not doing well, they're going to let you know. If you are doing well, they love you. Veterans Stadium was just a terrible place to play. The first year there, I struggled. The second year, I started off well. Then Anaheim wanted me, for my power."

Dealt at the trading deadline, Gant finished the 2000 season with the Angels. He spent '01 with Colorado and Oakland before signing with San Diego as a free agent and spending his last full big-league season in the warm southern California sun. A month into the 2003 season, Oakland, where Gant had returned as a free agent, released him. His playing days were over.

"And I started broadcasting," Gant said. "Early on in my career, some of the [broadcasters], the TBS guys, would interview me. They'd say, 'You ought to listen to yourself. You have a good voice. You could do this.' I did some postseason stuff for the Braves, and it started snowballing from there.

"I enjoy it," he said. "I get to be around the guys. I still get to be around the game."

Around the Braves, too. The first of eight big-league teams Gant played for, and still his team.

"I'm still a Brave, through and through," said Gant, who, with his wife, Heather, has four children. "Of course, I'm broadcasting for the Braves, but I want to remain with the Braves, and the organization.

"I helped turn this city around," he said. "I'm a Brave in my heart, and always will be. All I know is, I left my blood, my sweat, and my tears out on that field for the Braves."

GAME OF MY LIFE

"It has to be Game 7 of the '92 NLCS. Doug Drabek had pitched really well for the Pirates. I grew up around him. He's from Victoria, too [the Texas town about two hours south of Houston where Gant grew up]. He's two years older than me. He went to the private school, St. Joseph's. I went to Victoria High. We never played against each other—we were a Class 5-A school, they were 3-A—but I knew who he was. I remember him being really good in high school, and he was a damn good major-league pitcher.

"He pitched really well that night, and they had some momentum after winning the two previous games. They pretty much had it the whole game. But we stayed close. It was just one of those games that was just nail-biting from the first pitch to the last.

"After Terry Pendleton led off with a double, their second baseman, Jose Lind, made an error [on David Justice's grounder to

Lind's backhand]. That was what changed the game. Jose Lind didn't make errors. He was one of the best in the game. When that happened, it opened the door for us. It gives the other team a little bit of daylight, that we have a chance. When Drabek walked Sid Bream to load the bases, Stan Belinda came in to relieve. Then I hit a sacrifice fly to left.

"I knew I'd just missed it. When you hit 'em and you know it, that's one thing. But I did what I had to do—got the run in."

[After Damon Berryhill walked to re-load the bases, pinch hitter Brian Hunter popped out for the second out. Then pinch hitter Francisco Cabrera came to the plate.]

"I knew he was going to do it. He'd lined a pitch foul down the left-field line. He was on the pitch. When Cabrera hit it so hard to left, to [Barry] Bonds, I knew it was going to be a close play at the plate. Bonds was a Gold Glover, and we didn't have the fastest guy at second base. But Bonds had to go to his left to field the ball. If that ball's hit right at him, he throws Sid out by a mile. But he had to go to his left and then throw across his body. As soon as Sid slid, I knew he was safe.

"I almost beat Sid to home plate. I was standing on the top step of the dugout—we all were—and I just ran for the plate. It was just euphoric in the stadium. It was the loudest noise I'd ever heard in a stadium—still.

"It was a moment that was probably the most fun for me to see."

Chapter 9

GREG OLSON

"I had steak tonight," the voice said over the phone.

"Excuse me?"

"I had steak tonight."

And Lisa Olson and the caller, her husband's diarist, both laughed that long-ago Friday night.

In October of 1991, Lisa Olson's supper fare was not only fair game but must-read material each morning. That remarkable month, during the NLCS and World Series, her husband the catcher-turned-pitchman captivated Atlanta with his play and "Greg Olson's Playoff Diary." The sequel, "Greg Olson's World Series Diary," further regaled readers of the *Atlanta Journal-Constitution* with Oly's exploits and his endless stream of freebies. If it's free, it's Oly: Rental cars, Krispy Kremes, waterbeds, hotels, pizzas. You name it, Olson pitched it—daily, shamelessly, hilariously. Wisely, too. Has anyone in such a relatively brief major-league career ever capitalized so completely upon fame—and had such unabashed fun doing so?

"I was there at the right time," said Olson, who arrived in Atlanta in 1990 as a 29-year-old rookie, a minor-league lifer soon to turn 30 and seemingly bound for nowhere, and played four seasons. "The young guys, blue-chippers, have some time," Olson said. "I realized early I was going to have a limited amount of time. The Braves got hot and then opportunities were out there. Who knows why, but the city of Atlanta liked me.

"I was more of a blue collar-type player. I got my break and did well. I was always willing to sign the two, three, four more autographs. The fans just embraced me. I thought, 'If I don't take advantage of these opportunities now, I'll say, why didn't I do that?'

"It wasn't that I was money-hungry," he said. "I *liked* it. I'm a people person. I actually like doing that stuff."

Stuff like signing autographs at a sporting goods store one Saturday afternoon on a road trip, then playing that night. Two hours of scribbling and kibitzing, and here's your $3,000, thank you very much. Very good money for a bargain-basement catcher.

"That was my mentality," Olson said. "Do what you can at the time."

And oh, what Oly did in his brief tenure in Atlanta. "I played in one All-Star Game, two World Series, and three playoffs in a four-year period," he said. "You look back at some Hall of Fame players, they'd kill to play in one World Series."

In 1990, his first year in the Braves organization, Olson started out in Triple-A Richmond. Due to trades, retirements, injuries, and slumps, he wound up as the last man on Atlanta's roster, then Tom Glavine's catcher one game. "Glav said, 'Hey, I like the way this guy caught me. Let him catch me again,'" Olson said. "The pitchers liked throwing to me, plain and simple."

Somehow, Olson got hot at the plate early that season. He became the first Braves rookie since Ron Reed in '68 to make the NL All-Star team. In 1991, however, new general manager John Schuerholz acquired Mike Heath to catch. When Heath developed bone chips, Olson took over for good. "Once the machine got rolling," he said, "you're not going to change it."

After the All-Star break, Atlanta's worst-to-first odyssey mushroomed. Olson produced several clutch hits as the Braves chased

down the Dodgers. "That city was absolutely bazonkers," said Olson, who recalls being treated like "a prince." The crowds, once so meek and meager, were capacity and delirious. "It got to where a mouse couldn't get in because he'd get trampled," Olson said.

When Atlanta clinched the NL West on the next-to-last day of the season, Olson was photographically frozen in time: Leaping into the arms of "Schmoltzie." That's how Olson still pronounces the nickname of John Smoltz, the winning pitcher that day, Olson's close friend to this day. Not "Smoltzie," as everyone else pronounces it. "Schmoltzie." Schmaltzy? Nah. Not coming from Oly.

In the '91 NLCS, Olson led the Braves in batting (.333); he hit a two-run homer and even stole a base to beat Pittsburgh in Game 3. Olson held court afterward, and a teammate asked, "Who does he think he is, Johnny Bench?" Coach Pat Corrales replied, "He was today." Corrales knew: a career backup catcher, he once was stuck behind the Hall of Fame presence of one Johnny Bench.

"I don't think there's a day that goes by that some memory of '91 doesn't go through my head," Olson said. "A lot of baseball historians still say it was probably the best World Series ever."

In his native Minnesota, Olson was captured for posterity in Game 1 when Dan Gladden charged home and literally flipped Oly on his head. "I'll bet I sign 40 or 50 of those photos each year at Twins Fest," said Olson, now a successful realtor in the Minneapolis area. The more painful memories: Game 6, when Kirby Puckett's 11th-inning homer won it; Game 7, a magnificent pitching duel between Smoltz and Jack Morris until the Twins won 1-0 in the 10th.

"I still watch it on ESPN Classic," Olson said. "I'm hoping one of these days, somebody edits that thing and we score a run. And it *still* hasn't happened."

In 1992, Olson shared the catching duties with Damon Berryhill, but handled Atlanta's young pitchers superbly and again hit in the clutch. That September 18, however, he fractured his right leg and dislocated his ankle when Ken Caminiti bowled Olson over at the plate. He was carted off the field, wearing an air cast and a neck brace. Olson knew the neck brace would terrify his wife, watching on TV. To reassure Lisa, Oly, laying on his back, left the field doing the Tomahawk Chop.

"I'm just trying to tell my wife I'm okay," he said, "but everybody thinks this is golden."

The stadium erupted. Olson's season was done. In the ninth inning of Game 7 of the NLCS, Olson was in the dugout, wearing a thigh-to-ankle cast and on crutches, when Francisco Cabrera lined the two-out, two-run single that scored David Justice and Sid Bream and broke Pittsburgh's heart.

"Frankie hits the ball," Olson said, "and I throw down the crutches and start hopping out there on one leg. The adrenaline just flowed through me. All of a sudden, I was just gassed. I just laid down on the field."

Atlanta lost the World Series to Toronto. In '93, Olson essentially lost his starting job to Berryhill, and the Braves lost to Philadelphia in the NLCS in six games. With the youngster Javy Lopez ready in '94, the Braves didn't re-sign Olson; he went to spring training with the Mets, was released, and gladly went home to Minnesota.

"I thought, 'That's enough,'" Olson said. "And I had plenty to do." He had a young, growing family to care for. He got involved in real estate and prospered. Olson and Lisa now have three children— Ryan, Rachel, and Robbie. They live in Bear Path, a Jack Nicklaus development where Olson is a realtor in their golf community. He also spent two seasons managing the Minnesota Loons, a Single-A minor-league team with a pitcher named Kerry Ligtenberg—until, that is, Olson sold Ligtenberg to Atlanta, where he pitched from 1997-2002 and led the Braves with 30 saves in '98.

"I sold him for two dozen bats and a gross of balls," Olson said, laughing. "So Schuerholz once again got the best of me."

Yet no one got more out of less, or enjoyed and endeared himself more, than Oly the pitching catcher did in Atlanta.

"Timing is everything, isn't it?" he asked.

GAME OF MY LIFE

"Do you mean the game in which I played well, or the one I liked the best?" asks Olson. "For me, the game of my life was basically Game 7 of the '91 World Series.

"Throughout your childhood, how many times do you sit in the sandlot and think about playing in Game 7 of the World Series? As a kid, you always think, 'How would it be to play in Game 7?' But for me, to play in Game 7, in Minnesota, my hometown, against my hometown Twins, in perhaps the best and most exciting World Series ever, well, how can you get any better than that?

"Smoltz is pitching Game 7, he's virtually my best friend, me being the starting catcher, and I'm enjoying the game more than you could possibly imagine. People always ask me, 'How could you play, you being so nervous?' In Game 1, the first two innings, I could hardly feel the ball hit my mitt. The juices were flowing so much, and so intensely, I was numb. But after that, I just played.

"It was such an exceptional series . . . even though we came up one run short. Even though it was 0-0, and we're going into extra innings. The game had so much drama; so many things happened. To play in that game was undoubtedly the most important, best, and most pleasurable game ever.

"What jumps out at me the most would be how the Braves needed a run. [I don't fault] Lonnie Smith not scoring on that double by Terry Pendleton in the eighth inning. We still had the bases loaded. But Sid hit into a 3-2-3 double play, [Kent] Hrbek to home to first.

"You're sitting in the dugout, in the farthest corner of the bench. You want to jump up, you know you're going to score a run. And then they get a double play. Then the Twins have the bases loaded in the bottom of the eighth, but Stanton comes in, Hrbek hits a soft line drive to Lemke, who steps on second for a double play.

"In the bottom of the 10th, Dan Gladden leads off with a soft hit to center field. It bounced off the turf and over Ronnie Gant's head. Brian Hunter came over from left to come up with it, but Gladden gets a double and then they load the bases. Then my buddy Gene Larkin comes up to pinch hit. My good buddy Geno. We worked out together in the off-season. He comes to the plate and I say, 'Hey, Geno.' He won't say anything. I don't know if he was that nervous, or he just didn't hear me. But Geno's in the best situation you want to be in.

"He hits the first pitch from Alejandro Pena into left field, and it's over. I sat in the dugout for 10 minutes, saddened and watching the Twins. When I walked back up into the clubhouse, yes, it was a disappointing celebration, but what a season we'd had. Even though we came up one run short, we'd accomplished more than anybody expected. One team had to win, one team had to lose. We were the losers.

"I didn't see Geno again that night. After we lost, we went back to Atlanta for the parade, which was great. Then I drove up to Minnesota with a buddy in my Suburban. It was two or three weeks after Game 7 when I finally talked to Larkin. I said, 'Geno, how's it going?' I honestly forget what he said.

"After the World Series, Minnesota people were elated that the Twins had won their second World Series in five years. But the big emphasis wasn't on the closest played and perhaps the best World Series ever. It was the Halloween storm of '91, when they had 32 inches of snow. I recall being home only four or five days before this abominable 32-inch storm hit Minnesota. Thirty-two inches! It actually stopped the city for three full days. That never happens here.

"So that became the topic up here. And the celebration lasted less in Minnesota than it did in Atlanta.

"Now, the game that was the most important to me—the most important that I ever played in—was a Sunday game in Cincinnati early in the season in 1990. I wasn't even on the roster in 1990. But the day before the season started, Phil Lombardi quit. And that season, I got called up.

"That was the year with the [owners] lockout in spring training. So you started with 27 guys on the roster for the first month, not 25. The Braves had Jody Davis and Ernie Whitt to catch. With Lombardi quitting, I was the last guy on a 27-man roster. I had thought for sure they'd send me down and go with two catchers.

"The last game of the first week of the season, we were 1-5 or 1-6, and we were down 5 or 6-1. In the eighth inning, Russ Nixon, who was the manager then, called down to the bullpen and said, 'Hey, let Olson catch the ninth inning.' We scored four runs in the eighth and now it was a one-run game. Russ calls back and said, 'Tell Olson to hold on.' I'm sure Russ was thinking, 'We've got to win some games or I'm going to get fired.'

"That Saturday night, Nick Esasky gets hurt. He's scratched from the lineup Sunday. Tom Browning was pitching for the Reds Sunday, and Glavine was pitching for us. So Nixon puts Jody at first base, and I'm catching. I went 1-for-3, we won the game. Glav gave up one run and he liked the way I caught him.

"So, the next time Glavine pitched, he wanted me to catch. I went 3-for-4, with my first major-league home run. The most important thing was, I got a chance to play. If I don't, I probably get sent down. But I got another chance to play, got a hit, and we won. From then on, I started hitting more.

"I was hitting, like, .370. Jody Davis was hitting, like, a buck-fifty. Two days later, Ernie Whitt broke his thumb on a play at the plate. I end up playing in the All-Star Game. I go from almost being cut, a guy quits, a guy gets hurt, and I get a chance, to being in the All-Star Game. Somebody had to be picked from the Braves, so Roger Craig—who was managing San Francisco then—picked me. The game was played in Wrigley Field. Mike Scioscia caught most of the game. I caught the last two innings and got to hit.

"Chuck Finley of the Angels was pitching. He threw strike one called, then strike two called. I said, 'I'm not going down without a swing.' Then Finley threw me a nasty forkball and I swung and missed."

To this day, Olson keeps in touch with his old '91 World Series battery mate, "Schmoltzie." Olson followed Smoltz and the Braves through their stretch of division championships.

"I think it's very unfortunate that the Braves could only win one World Series." Olson said. "They're going to be remembered as the team that won 14 straight titles but won just one World Series. But that may be a benchmark that may never be reached again.

"It makes me very proud to know I was there at the beginning, at the early stages of rebuilding before the streak began. You have to give a lot of credit to Bobby Cox."

And Nixon, who gave Oly his shot.

Chapter 10

PETE VAN WIEREN

For a kid who somehow overcame his eighth-grade teacher's vocational advice to become an optician, for a guy who never quite bathed in the bright broadcasting lights of Rochester, New York, Pete Van Wieren's done all right for himself. Don'tcha think?

"The best play-by-play man in America," says Don Sutton, the Hall of Fame pitcher-turned-broadcaster and formerly Van Wieren's on-air partner for Atlanta Braves broadcasts.

"I hate the S.O.B.," said Skip Caray, Van Wieren's broadcast colleague for nearly three decades who was inducted into the Braves Hall of Fame with Van Wieren in 2004. "He's a hell of an announcer. He should have been a network announcer full-time."

"A lot of times, you hear announcers trying to be funny, or trying to degrade players," said Tom Glavine, the two-time NL Cy Young winner who spent his first 15 big-league seasons with Atlanta before opting for free agency with the New York Mets. "Pete doesn't do any of that. He doesn't get into criticizing players a lot, if at all. It's not his style. But when he does, it means something."

For 32 seasons, Van Wieren has meant one thing to his audience: on-air professionalism and excellence. "The Professor," Ernie Johnson called Van Wieren soon after hiring him in 1976. Ever since, Van Wieren's been a walking, talking baseball encyclopedia, one of the most industrious and prepared, effective and educational broadcasters extant.

"When I got in this business, what I really wanted to do was become the broadcaster for the Rochester Red Wings," Van Wieren said of that longtime Baltimore Triple-A affiliate. "I'm from Rochester, and I thought that was the best job in the world. I never got it.

"But when I went around to the other minor-league places where I worked—Binghamton and Toledo, and especially Tidewater—the general managers I was associated with, every one of them urged me to aim a little higher."

He hit the heights in 1976 when Atlanta hired him. "It was the major leagues," Van Wieren said. At least, technically. "I'd been doing minor leagues all those years. Just being able to go to all the major-league ballparks, face major-league teams, and have a major-league atmosphere and environment, that was good enough. I didn't care whether we won or lost or whatever."

Good thing: From 1975-79, Atlanta lost between 92 and 101 games annually. After brief success under Bobby Cox and Joe Torre, the Braves suffered six abysmal seasons from 1985-90, breaking the 70-win barrier once and going 54-106 in '88.

"That stretch from 1976 to '90, basically—how do I say this?— you almost didn't feel like you were part of the major leagues," Van Wieren said. "The World Series was something other people went to.

"We had that one little taste of the playoffs in '82, but it was three-and-out. The transformation, to go from a [terrible] team like that, for all those years, to a team that was in the postseason every year since 1991 through 2005 is remarkable."

"The most remarkable year of all." That's what Van Wieren calls Atlanta's otherworldly worst-to-first miracle of '91, when the Braves won the pennant and captivated the city with the "Tomahawk Chop," beat Pittsburgh in the NLCS, and lost an epic World Series Game 7 in Minnesota, 1-0.

"Nothing will ever top that one," he said. "You had no clue if that was going to happen again, or if it was a one-time deal."

After flying back to Atlanta after Game 2 that October, Van Wieren was aboard a bus carrying some National League executives. Behind him sat Jay Horwitz, the Mets vice-president of media relations.

"In his New York accent," Van Wieren recalled, "Jay said, 'This seems so bizarre to be coming to a World Series in At-*lan*-ta.' I sat there chuckling and thinking, 'Yes, it does seem bizarre, but it sure is fun.'

"No one expected it," he said. "But then it became a regular thing. For 15 years, going into spring training, the mind-set has been expecting to win the World Series. It makes our job much easier."

A week after Van Wieren got the job, Ted Turner bought the Braves. The announcers—and often the new owner—took part in on-field ostrich races and cow chip-throwing contests. Van Wieren soon added the title of traveling secretary, doing double duty for several seasons, making travel and hotel arrangements for the Braves.

On May 11, 1977 in Pittsburgh, on the day Turner managed the team for one game, Van Wieren had to hail a cab at the team hotel, then serve as the lookout while highly embarrassed manager Dave Bristol slipped unnoticed into the taxi and sped off to the airport before any Braves could see him. At the ballpark later that afternoon, Van Wieren was sitting in the visiting manager's office when Turner summoned the coaches and announced their new duties. Van Wieren recalled that pitching coach Johnny Sain, "who may have been the only person in Pittsburgh who didn't know what was going on, asked, 'Where's Dave?' He had no clue."

Of course, neither did Turner. The Braves lost 2-1, extending their losing streak to 17 games. Afterwards, Van Wieren remembered, Turner was hungry and set off in search of a meal. No restaurants were open at that hour of the night. Finally, Turner found a little pizzeria, a hole-in-the-wall joint. The owner ordered a slice of pizza and a glass of wine. The waitress returned shortly, Van Wieren said, "With a little square of pizza and wine in what looked like a cordial glass." Turner's response was predictable and vintage Ted. "He said, 'What's this?'"

Van Wieren recalled, laughing. "'I didn't come here for communion. Bring me some pizza and wine!' Now *that* was a fun day."

Even if Van Wieren's first 15 seasons in the major leagues weren't. During the early years of that awful stretch, Van Wieren relished the professionalism and tenacity of Phil Niekro, the popular Hall of Fame knuckleballer who won 316 games, but rued that some teammates lacked his focus and desire to win. Come 1991, though, everything changed. During that '91 pennant race and postseason, Van Wieren arrived at Atlanta-Fulton County Stadium early each day, walked the concourse that encircled the dank, old multipurpose ballpark, and savored the hysteria in the parking lots.

"There were tomahawks everywhere, all kinds," he said. "There were Indians beating the drums, then Indian protestors in the postseason. I didn't want to miss it. And then, to get to the World Series, and have it be so great. . . ."

Van Wieren recalls Lonnie Smith, leading off Game 7 ("the ultimate game") in the Metrodome, walking to home plate and shaking hands with Twins catcher Brian Harper. Later, Smith was deked and didn't score from first on a double, a blunder many believe cost Atlanta the series.

"But then you had the Sid Bream double play—pitcher to home to first," Van Wieren said. "Even after the Lonnie Smith baserunning mistake, you still had a chance to score. And the night before was even more unfortunate, the Kirby Puckett homer off Charlie Leibrandt in the 12th inning of Game 6.

"And then the Braves finally won in '95," he said. "And just to be in the World Series in 1996, at Yankee Stadium. There had been so many games there when you were growing up, watching [Series] games on TV, and almost every year they were at Yankee Stadium. To finally be a part of that was great.

"So, have I done everything in my career?" asked Pete Van Wieren. "I guess the answer would probably, amazingly be yes. I don't know what else I could have ever expected to do."

How about induction into the Braves Hall of Fame? Van Wieren's sons were on hand that afternoon, along with his wife, Elaine, and his mother. In his remarks after being inducted, Van Wieren told the audience about Chipper Jones' comments immediately after hitting a game-winning home run, hearing the crowd's roar, realizing what he'd accomplished and the wonder of it all.

"I just wish everybody could experience this feeling," Van Wieren recalled Jones saying.

He paused. Then Van Wieren told the third baseman, sitting with all his teammates in the audience, "Chipper, now I know how you felt."

GAME OF MY LIFE

"Do I have to pick just one?" asks Van Wieren. "There was the seventh game of the 1991 World Series. The [NL West Division] clinching game in '91. Ted Turner managing that game in Pittsburgh in '77. And the very first Braves game I did, 1976. After you've worked in the minors all those years, and you finally get a job in the major leagues, the longest period of time in your life is the time from when you get the job and that first major-league game you do. My first game was going to be a spring training game against the Dodgers.

"You think, 'My goodness, my first game is going to be with Steve Garvey and Davey Lopes and Ron Cey. Well, that spring was the [owners] lockout. For Turner, it was his first game, too, that first Saturday in spring training. And he was bound and determined to televise a baseball game that day. Ted had all these non-roster players. Bill Veeck, who owned the White Sox, had them, too. So we ended up broadcasting a game from Sarasota, and it was with the same minor-league guys I'd done all my life.

"Instead of Davey Lopes or Ron Cey or Steve Garvey, my first batter was Jorge Aranzamendi. I'll never forget that. He was an infielder. I knew these guys better than Ernie did! Geez, you dream and dream and dream about that first major-league game, and that's what it turns out to be. The whole atmosphere was, well, I'd been with Tidewater for several years and the White Sox had a couple of guys who'd been with Tidewater. Rich Puig was a second baseman. Cleon Jones, who was once the Mets' left fielder, had been in the Mets camp. But my very first batter, leading off for the Braves, was Jorge

Aranzamendi. Let's see, he played that year in . . . let me check. I've got a database with all the major-league and minor-league players."

[Van Wieren, ever the baseball statistician, historian and authority, logged onto his computer, called up the database, and found his man. Found the correct spelling for Aranzamendi, too.]

"He wound up starting that year in the Southern League, with the Savannah Braves.

"Now, the very first regular-season game I did, we opened up the '76 season in San Diego. Carl Morton pitched for the Braves and Randy Jones for San Diego. [Van Wieren recalls this immediately and exactly, right off the top of his bald head]. We lost 8-2.

"There were only three of us then: Skip, myself, and Ernie. They were doing TV and I was by myself on the radio side. That was, well, not intimidating, but there was a lot going on. The opener was on a Friday, and that was the weekend Andy Messersmith signed with the Braves as a free agent.

"I'm over there by myself on radio. I think, 'Wow! This is the big leagues, the first real game where the fans can catch me!' I don't want the fans to say, 'Who's this jerk?'

"My first batter was Rowland Office, the Braves' leadoff hitter in the first inning. He walked. Here's Rowland Office, my first hitter in the big leagues, and he walked against Randy Jones, one of the best control pitchers of all time.

"The good ol' Braves made four errors that day, and we got beat 8-2. It was a little different 15 years later in '91. What I remember most about the '91 season is there was the buildup that whole year, and the way the town went nuts. For the first time since I'd been in Atlanta since '76, the town was nuts over baseball in October. There was the Tomahawk Chop and all that stuff going on around town.

"The Braves were chasing the Dodgers and Tommy Lasorda. I remember Darryl Strawberry saying, 'Hey, it's only the Braves, we're not worried about them.' On the next to the last day of the season, Saturday, October 5, we beat Houston 5-2. It was Smoltz, he went the distance, and once Justice caught a fly ball to right for the final out, Olson jumped into Smoltz's arms. But we'd only clinched a tie for first. The Dodgers were still playing the Giants.

"So we stayed on the air. After they'd ran on the field to celebrate, everybody on the team gathered out by the mound to watch the end of the Dodgers-Giants game. It was almost the sense of broadcasting your own game, you're letting the radio audience know what's happening.

"But it was a strange thing. Once you had the celebration, with Smoltz and Olson, then things calmed down a bit, then you watched the Giants beat the Dodgers, and then you had to have a double celebration. That was unique.

"After the fact, I heard all kinds of stories. My sons, Jon and Steve, were coming back from a Georgia football game, and they were listening on the radio. They told me after the last out was made, all the people on the highway leaving the Georgia game started honking their horns and waving little Braves flags.

"There will never be another season like '91."

Chapter 11

SKIP CARAY

O ver the last three decades, he's made some of the most memorable play-by-play calls in Atlanta Braves history. But what's Skip Caray's best call? You make the call.

Can you conjure up a crisp October World Series evening in 1995? "Fly ball, deep left-center! . . . Grissom on the run . . . Yes! Yes! Yes! The Atlanta Braves have given you a world championship! Listen to this crowd!"

Some Braves fans still listen to this call to this day. Every time they open a beer with a certain bottle opener, it replays the call when activated by popping the top on a cold one. Top of the ninth, bottoms up. Cheers!

"A mob scene on the field! The Atlanta Braves have brought the first championship to Atlanta!"

With sincere apologies to Hank Aaron and No. 715, do you recall the single most dramatic moment in Braves history? Two outs in the ninth inning, Game 7 of the 1992 NLCS, Pittsburgh up 2-1. And here's Skip: "A double, an error, and a walk, and the bases are full of

Braves. Bream carries the winning run . . . two balls, one strike. What tension . . . the runners lead. A lotta room in right-center. If he hits one there, we can dance in the streets. The 2-1 . . .

"Swing—*line drive left field!* One run is in! Here comes Bream, here's the throw to the plate. He *iiiiiiiiiisssssssss . . . safe!* Braves win! Braves win! Braves win! Braves win!"

Pause.

"Braves win!"

If you're from Atlanta, you know that Skip screamed "Braves win!" five heavenly times. Not three times. Not four. But five—after pausing.

Remember a day at the races in Atlanta-Fulton County Stadium in the late '70s? The ostrich races, when Skip Caray and the Braves neophyte owner, Ted Turner, were jockeys—wearing silks and all—in a pregame ostrich race. What did Caray call Turner? "#$%&+@*!"

Seems Caray, trailing in the race around the field's perimeter because "I had a slow, dumb ostrich," suddenly veered his trusty fowl from center field straight toward home plate. He won. Turner screamed, "You cheated! You cheated!" To which Caray replied, "How can I cheat? It's a freakin' ostrich!"

He now admits, "I cheated my tail off. Man, that was fun."

So, Skip Caray's best call of all time? It first surfaced in 2005, his 30th season calling Braves baseball, and continued for two seasons. It's simply, "Partner." As in, "We go to the top of the third, and here's my broadcast partner, Chip Caray."

"Thanks, Dad. Chipper Jones leads it off for the Braves. . . ."

He's 67 now. Imagine that. Skip Caray, Harry's boy, 67. Eligible for full Social Security benefits. Not that he needs them, mind you. Yet Harry's been gone since 1998, and still there's an ache in Skip's heart. But now his oldest son, Chip, who made his own name for himself with WGN and the Cubs, has joined the Braves broadcast team on Turner Sports. Now in their third season, father and son talk Atlanta Braves baseball on the air. Nice. How nice?

"As a father and a broadcaster," Skip said, "I'm just thrilled to death."

Healthier than he's been in several years, too. Re-energized by the Braves' unexpected run to a 13th consecutive division title in 2004,

then a 14th in '05 before the unparalleled string finally ended last season, Caray was reinvigorated, too. "I must say, I feel better [physically] than I have in a long time," he said. "The pacemaker has helped a lot."

Hospitalized over the 2003 Thanksgiving holiday, Caray had a pacemaker implanted that Friday. "It's not major surgery, but they're still [messing] with your heart," he recalled. "That was a long 48 hours. I did a lot of thinking."

On New Year's Eve, 2000, he'd marked the advent of the 21st century by giving up drinking. "I thought I'd take a centennial off, then come back stronger than ever," Caray said, laughing. "I thought all the computers were going to go off with Y2K, and so was I. Honestly, I think I went through the college football [bowls] and had a few cocktails. I mean, let's not get silly about this. But it was easier than quitting smoking, and that's been 21 years. I wish I'd done it years ago."

In August of 2004—Friday the 13th, actually—Caray sat with his wife, Paula, and youngest son, Josh, amid an overflow luncheon crowd in the 755 Club at Turner Field. It should have been one of the very best days of Caray's life. Joe Simpson, Caray's on-air broadcast partner and the emcee that afternoon, told the crowd that Skip had turned 65 the previous day and would everyone care to sing along with Joe? Nearly 500 people crooned, "Happy Birthday" to Caray. It was a terrific way to open the club's annual Braves Hall of Fame induction luncheon. Caray was one of four inductees, along with his longtime on-air broadcast partner, Pete Van Wieren. At the start of the 2003 season, the two great announcers had been humbled—and deeply hurt—when AOL Time Warner, the new Braves ownership, relegated them to radio and regional broadcasts on Turner South.

Simpson and Don Sutton, meanwhile, were paired on TBS broadcasts across the country. Viewers who'd tuned in to Pete and Skip for years on Ted Turner's Superstation couldn't watch them anymore. The fan outcry was immediate and furious. Management relented. Skip and Pete returned to TBS. "Yes, it was hurtful," Caray said. "But on the flip side, there are nights when I drive home and I say, 'I wonder if anybody gives a damn? Does what I do have any meaning at all?' I think we all have those moments in our lives, of introspection or whatever you want to call it. What Pete and I found out is, a lot of people do care.

"That was very rewarding," he said. "I'll never forget that as long as I live. What started out as a bummer turned out to be a very nice experience at the end. . . . Some of the people really missed us. That's very gratifying."

Many of those people attended the Braves Hall of Fame luncheon. When he was inducted, Caray opened his remarks in, well, vintage Skip fashion. He told an off-color joke. Got a big laugh, too. Then he spoke of his family, of his longtime colleague Van Wieren and their mentor, Ernie Johnson. Then Skip Caray grew serious.

"If you are people who pray, a prayer for Chris Caray would be very much appreciated right now," he said. "Because the odds are stacked against him."

As Skip spoke, Chris, his younger brother, lay terminally ill in a St. Louis hospital. Chris had been diagnosed with an inoperable brain tumor. On the Sunday prior to his Braves Hall of Fame luncheon, Skip had left the Braves in Arizona and flown to St. Louis to be by his brother's bedside. When he arrived at the hospital, Chris was very disoriented.

"One of the last things he said was, 'Isn't Skip's hall of fame thing about to happen?'" Caray said after the induction ceremony. "That assured me my place was here." In Atlanta. His sister-in-law Diana begged him, so Skip flew home from St. Louis on his 65th birthday to attend the event.

"One of Chris' goals was to be here," Caray said that Friday, just a day after returning from St. Louis. "It's a strange day in that your heart is so full on one hand, and then so empty on the other. I've never been afraid of making a speech in my life, but today I was."

He spoke eloquently. Gratefully. At times, hilariously. He talked of baseball, and good fortune and family. The next day, Chris died. He was 57. Skip flew to St. Louis for the funeral, then returned home and went back on the air, doing what he's always done: He called a good game. Made some caustic remarks, resurrected an old clever one, too ("And there's another double for Andruw Jones. . ."), and returned the favor to all those fans who wanted Skip and Pete back on TBS—and got their wish.

Now, four decades after re-creating Tulsa Oilers road games on KVOO radio, using the Western Union ticker for pitch-by-pitch updates and striking a little square piece of balsa wood with a pencil to simulate the crack of the bat, Caray still followed in his famous father's Hall of Fame footsteps. His oldest son having joined him in the booth, now Josh is even embarking on a career in broadcasting, too. Imagine father and two sons, all working together.

Caray recalls his greatest thrills in sports, and they may surprise you. "Without question," he said, "Chip hit a grand slam to win a Little League game when he was six years old, and I was his coach. I had tears pouring down my face. It was like I had the flu and I was shaking so bad, I was so excited. With Josh, it was watching him play [football] his senior year at Lovett. They got beat in a playoff game, but it was the best game of his life. He had 16, 18 tackles. Just played his butt off.

"Nothing against these great athletes I've gotten to watch," Skip Caray said. "But your kids, boy, that's something special."

What made Father's Day 2005 so memorable for Caray was his kid, his boy, the eldest, working beside him that Sunday afternoon in Cincinnati. They couldn't recall the last time they'd spent a Father's Day in each other's company. And Chip couldn't forget that awful day 35 years earlier.

"The day my parents officially split up," he recalled. "I remember Dad going away."

Chip, then 5, and his younger sister, Cindy, were living with their parents Lila and Skip in Chamblee, a suburb of Atlanta. Skip was the Atlanta Hawks' bon vivant broadcaster, and his marriage to Lila had not been good for a long time. Chip still recalls, vividly and painfully, the day his father drove away from their home. As Skip's car started down the road, Chip asked, "Mom, where's Daddy going?"

To this day, Chip remembers her reply: "My mom said, 'He's going on a long road trip.' You think, 'Okay.' You never think that he's not coming back. Ten days might as well be a year."

Ten days became an eternity. Skip never returned home from that road trip; he and Lila had already decided to divorce, after a loud, angry fight the night before that the children had accidentally witnessed.

"That trip lasted the rest of our lives," Skip now says. "You feel like you've failed your children. That's the biggest failure of my life."

Caray carries the guilt to this day, largely because of his own childhood trauma. Skip was six, maybe seven, that morning he walked to school in Webster Groves, a suburb of St. Louis where Harry was already a wildly popular broadcaster with the Cardinals. On the walk to school that morning, Skip spied the front-page headline in the old *St. Louis Globe-Democrat*: "Caray's Wife Tunes Him Out," it read.

"Longest walk of my life," Skip now recalls. "People staring at me like I had two heads."

That pain, that longing for his father—at 8:30 each night during Cardinals broadcasts, Harry would say, "We pause for station identification. Good night, Skip. This is the Cardinals' baseball network"—made Skip so sympathetic to Chip's own divorced parents' plight. It's why finally getting to work with his first-born became such a pure joy and parental second chance.

And it's why Skip's choice for his "Game of My Life" was so easy, so apt. Perfectly so.

GAME OF MY LIFE

"I think the best game I ever broadcast was the Bream-Cabrera thing on radio. Rick Shaw was the producer for WSB then, and he later presented me with a tape of the ninth inning of the game. I have to admit it's the best work I've ever done. And Marquis catching the fly ball to win the World Series in '95 was great. I was lucky enough to be on the air for both of those golden moments.

"But the game that Dad and Chip and I did at Wrigley Field was unforgettable, and my most memorable. It was on May 13, 1991, and it was the first time three generations of broadcasters from one family had ever worked together.

"All we did was one opening [segment] together on the field, and both stations used it. We went by seniority all the way; Dad started, then I talked, and then Chip. Then Dad went over to the WGN booth and we went over to TBS and did the game. But God, the media attention and the hype were incredible.

"We stayed at a hotel near Dad's restaurant, Harry Caray's. Chip was working for SportSouth then for Turner. We were walking over to the restaurant for a one o'clock press conference. We were going to meet Dad there, and all of a sudden there were cameramen walking backward to shoot us.

"I said, 'God, now I know how John Gotti feels!' There were all these camermen walking backwards, filming us. Just a fat guy and a good-looking kid walking, and their cameras are all over us. I thought, 'You've gotta be kidding me.'

"At the press conference at the park, it was the same thing. Just a media horde. I'll never forget, Tom Glavine was pitching that game, and he asked me, 'What the hell's going on?' I told him, 'My Dad and son and I are working together, and that's never happened before in broadcasting.'

"Glav said, 'Well, that's really neat. That being the case, I'd better pitch you guys a little classic.' And he did—pitched a three-hit gem. Tom and I have been friends for a long time, and just the thought of knowing he pitched well was so nice.

"But before the game, there were so many people around. So many players were around, too. I remember seeing [Greg] Olson and [John] Smoltz watching the three of us, and laughing. And I went over and said, 'If I ever criticize you guys for the way you treat the media, shoot me.'

"After that, and other than Glavine, I have no remembrance of the game at all."

Chapter 12

LONNIE SMITH

H e didn't see the play. Lonnie Smith wasn't watching television in October of 2004, during the Boston-St. Louis World Series, when Cardinals pitcher Jeff Suppan was caught off third base and off guard, then tagged out. Smith didn't see any of the subsequent TV footage of famous World Series gaffes, either. He didn't have to.

"Did they show my play?" Smith asked, chuckling.

They did, indeed. Along with Johnny Pesky holding the ball and Bill Buckner allowing a slow roller to slip between his legs, Lonnie Smith's baserunning blunder in Game 7 of the 1991 World Series has become a Fall Classic misadventure. An autumnal perennial.

"They always show it, because it's part of history," said the ex-Braves outfielder long known as "Skates," because it occasionally appeared as if he was ice skating while trying to run down fly balls in the outfield. "I didn't respond to the media [after that game], and they didn't like that.

"Some things—good and bad—are destined to be part of history," Smith continued. "Those of us who are part of the bad things have to deal with it. Those who are the cause of good things reap the benefits.

"But that definitely will be the one associated with me, the one they remember and show."

Braves broadcaster Pete Van Wieren has another Lonnie Smith memory from that game. "It's the only time I've ever seen a Game 7 begin with a player, Lonnie Smith, walking up and shaking hands with Brian Harper, the Twins catcher," said Van Wieren. "I thought that was great."

In the eighth inning of that scoreless, breathless Game 7, Smith led off with a single. In the indoor pandemonium of the Metrodome in Minneapolis, with Terry Pendleton at bat, Smith tried a delayed steal. As he ran toward second, "The mistake I made was [that] I didn't take a peek in," Smith said. "I didn't know where the ball was."

"If anybody wants to blame me for anything," he said, "blame me for not looking in at the batter."

Hadn't Smith already homered in Games 3, 4, and 5 (the first National Leaguer to do so in Series history)? More important, hadn't he overcome his drug addiction in the mid-'80s to save his life, much less resurrect his career? Shouldn't a baserunning blunder, even in the Series, pale beside that?

"There are [baseball] mistakes made day in and day out. But especially in the World Series, if you make one, people remember," said Smith, the first player to appear in the World Series with four different teams—Philadelphia, St. Louis, Kansas City, and Atlanta.

In the white handkerchief-waving din of the Metrodome, Smith never picked up the ball off Pendleton's bat. He said he wasn't deked by Twins second baseman Chuck Knoblauch. Smith looked toward the outfield and saw centerfielder Kirby Puckett and left fielder Dan Gladden converging toward left-center.

Smith has watched the videotape many times, and told his wife, Dorothy, "I didn't recall myself stopping at second. I thought I hesitated. But she said I did stop."

He did, not knowing if the ball would be caught. When Smith saw it hit the wall, he took off for third base, where coach Jimy Williams held him up.

"Why he stopped, I just don't know," Braves manager Bobby Cox said afterward.

"We should have won the game and we should be world champions," said general manager John Schuerholz.

Yet Atlanta still had runners at second and third, nobody out. "Nobody pays attention to that," Smith recalled.

What everyone remembers is how Ron Gant weakly grounded out; how David Justice was intentionally walked before Sid Bream bounced into a 3-2-3 double play to end the inning; how the Twins scored in the bottom of the 10th to win 1-0 and deny Atlanta its first world championship.

"If I'd known we wouldn't score, I'd have tried to steal home," Smith said, laughing. "Not that I'd have made it. I guess people all think I should have scored on Terry's double. If you don't know where the ball is at, you can't be running blindly."

Smith won World Series rings with Philadelphia (1980), St. Louis (1982), and Kansas City (1985). He appeared in two more World Series with the Braves in '91 and '92. When Atlanta didn't re-sign him, Smith played two seasons with Pittsburgh and Baltimore before retiring in 1995. Ask what he's doing nowadays, and Smith replies, "Nothing, mostly. Just trying to be a father and husband.

"It's a little tougher than when I was playing. Takes a lot more practice," he said, laughing. Smith and his second wife, Dorothy, live in Fayetteville, 15 miles south of Atlanta, with their three daughters. He's a happy house husband and father.

"I'm fortunate that I don't have to work," said Smith, who turned 51 three days before Christmas. He has his savings and investments. Smith was awarded $1.75 million in collusion settlements, for money he lost in the free-agent markets of 1986 and '87 due to collusion by major-league owners. That also speaks to his one-time distance from the Braves. For several years, Smith stayed away from the game and Turner Field. In 2002, at his wife's urging, he accepted an invitation to attend an autograph session at the ballpark. Smith was warmly welcomed by Cox and his ex-teammates, and returned again in 2003. But Smith, who's considered going into coaching, didn't see a game at Turner Field in the 2004 season.

"I still have the desire to coach," he said. "It's trying to make the commitment, set up interviews, and contact people. My wife still wants me to be at home. I love being at home, but part of me wants to get back into the game."

"It's not easy to get back in once you're out," Smith said. "Most of the people I know aren't in it any more, other than the Braves. But I don't have a very good one-on-one relationship with John Schuerholz, so my chances of getting back into it with the Braves aren't that good."

Schuerholz was the Royals' general manager in 1985 when Smith was acquired from St. Louis. That September, Smith testified—in exchange for immunity—at the trial of his former drug dealer, Curtis Strong, the Pirates' former clubhouse caterer who dealt to ballplayers. Smith was fined and punished by Major League Baseball. Schuerholz discouraged him from protesting his punishment by MLB. Smith was angered even more when Schuerholz wanted him to re-sign for less than half of his 1986 salary. Smith became a free agent, received no other offers, and suspected collusion.

After being released following the '87 season, there were again no offers. His agent told Smith that Schuerholz had badmouthed him, that his attitude was poor and he could no longer play. That off-season, Smith told Carroll Rogers of the *Atlanta Journal-Constitution*, Smith bought a pistol and fired it into the ground in his backyard, to gauge the recoil if and when Smith took the gun to Kansas City and shot Schuerholz.

"I was at a point where I didn't care about a lot of things," Smith told Rogers. "I didn't care if I spent the rest of my life in jail or dead."

Instead, he found work in Atlanta in '88 when Cox, then the general manager, offered him a minor-league contract. Smith also met Dorothy Driver late that season, after he'd been called up to Atlanta and became the Braves regular left fielder. The following year, Smith was named the NL Comeback Player of the Year after hitting a career-high 21 homers with 79 RBIs.

Now, nearly two decades later, Smith's at peace with himself. He has a good relationship with his children from his first marriage, son Tramaine, 27, and daughter Sissy, 26. He delights in his daughters with Dorothy: Kayla, 14, Kendra, 12, and Kionna, 8.

"With the girls now," Smith said, "I want to spend as much time with them as possible, as much of their life as possible."

And long after hesitating at second in the Metrodome, Lonnie Smith is safely, happily at home.

GAME OF MY LIFE

"The one that stands out almost more to me than any other is the day I hit a grand slam off Nolan Ryan. It wasn't a game with the Braves. I was a Cardinal at the time. I can't even remember much about the game outside of the home run. I know it was a grand slam, and I think the year was 1982. It was against Nolan Ryan, and that's about it."

[The game was actually on August 31, 1984, at Busch Stadium. Smith, hitting fifth in the lineup that day, took Ryan deep for a grand slam in the first inning.]

"I was lucky that game," Smith continued. "I think he tried to throw me a changeup. I don't think it was a fastball.

"I never really had problems batting against him. I think it was the only extra base hit I had off Ryan, but I had a lot of hits—singles—off him."

[In his career, Smith actually batted .500 against Ryan with a double, a home run, ten singles, five walks, and two hit-by-pitches.]

"I guess because I came up [to the big leagues] as a leadoff hitter, I stood close to the plate. I saw a lot of fastballs. Nolan really kept it down and away. But the one time I hit [the grand slam], the pitch was up and a changeup.

"When I faced Ryan, I was always geared up—being young and anxious to prove myself. I never did get a chance to face J.R. Richard of the Astros. Don Sutton always got me with his breaking stuff. I faced Vida Blue, too, but not when he was a kid with Oakland. Later on, when he was with the Giants.

"With Ryan, his fastball just exploded. Facing him, and facing Bob Welch of the Dodgers, was kind of the same thing. Bob Welch usually stayed up high, though. But Ryan, if he threw his fastball and it was down, it was impossible to hit.

"There were a number of tough pitchers when I came up. Ryan probably was the toughest and fastest, even though I also faced Sutton,

Welch, Burt Hooton. A lot of those guys had good arms and were good pitchers.

"I need to throw in the Niekro Brothers, Phil and Joe, as tough pitchers, too. And Charlie Hough. I think they were the toughest knuckleballers. Nowadays, people think Tim Wakefield is. I'm not taking anything away from him, but I thought the Niekro Brothers were really tough to hit. And Hough, too. Even Tom Candiotti, too. The Niekro Brothers, and Tom Candiotti, would mix in a fastball.

"Then there were relievers like Joe Sambito of Houston and Pittsburgh's Kent Tekulve. And Rick Reuschel. I was lucky enough to face them, and get a few hits off them. But it wasn't easy. That's why I was a slap hitter. I had to be a slap-hitting leadoff hitter. I wasn't the best fielder, but I could run when I was young. As I got older and the role got tougher, I became more of a power hitter. I always stayed close to the plate, but I opened my stance up.

"My first year with St. Louis in 1982, my first hit as a Cardinal was a grand slam on Opening Day [at Busch Stadium] off [the Pirates'] Rick Rhoden after striking out a couple of times. I dropped a fly ball for an error, and I struck out my first two times at bat. My third time, I hit a grand slam.

"But I remember that grand slam off Nolan Ryan most."

✳ ✳ ✳

Smith misses the game a great deal. While he attends some Braves functions now, he says he doesn't feel comfortable going into the clubhouse.

"I do try to say hello to the guys I know," said Smith, whose only one-time Braves teammate still with the club is John Smoltz. "I say hi to Bobby [Cox] and the coaches and Terry [Pendleton, a one-time teammate of Smith's in St. Louis, and later Atlanta's third baseman in the early 1990s when Smith was a Braves outfielder]. But I'm a civilian now.

"I still get the chills and the excitement now going back to the ballpark."

Smith, who batted .288 in a 17-year major-league career and hit 98 home runs, still holds out hope for a return to the game.

"I don't want to manage so much, but rather coach," Smith said. "Even though I'd love to be in the big leagues, I think it'd be better coaching in the minors, helping kids develop. In the minors, that's where a lot of your friendships in the game started.

"The travel stunk," he said, laughing, "but they now have some great ballparks in the minors. Yes, I'd like to get back in the game and coach."

Chapter 13

HENRY AARON

Customers who shopped and bought at Hank Aaron BMW, in the Atlanta suburb of Union City, were sometimes startled to see the majority owner himself hand over an autographed baseball or book, along with the keys to a newly purchased Beamer. But then, Henry Louis Aaron took to business nearly as successfully as he took to turning on a fastball. Indeed, in his 70s, life is very, very good for "The Hammer," baseball's all-time home run king.

"Oh, yes, I'm enjoying myself," said Aaron. "For the first time, in the last few years, I think I've had more fun than in a long time. I'm more comfortable with myself.

"I can go out to all places, not just some places, and be a normal person," he said. "At least most times, I can. I think people respect me a little more. They leave me alone more than they used to.

"Life has been very good to me," said "Bad Henry," as Sandy Koufax and Don Drysdale liked to call Aaron once the Dodgers had abandoned the borough of Brooklyn for the untapped wealth of Los

Angeles. "They say good things come to those who wait, and I've waited a long time."

It's been 41 years now since Hank Aaron, the third of eight children of a Mobile, Alabama, dockworker, came home to the South. In 1966, the Milwaukee Braves moved to Atlanta, bringing major-league sports to the Deep South and baseball's best player back home to his Southern roots. Eight seasons later, at 9:07 p.m. on the crisp evening of April 8, 1974, Aaron broke the most hallowed record in all of sports. Before a sellout crowd of 53,775 in Atlanta-Fulton County Stadium, with a huge national television audience tuned in, he turned on an Al Downing fastball and lined it over the left-field fence and into the Los Angeles Dodgers bullpen. There, Braves reliever Tom House caught the historic ball. With that, his 715th career home run, Aaron surpassed Babe Ruth as baseball's home run king.

You've seen the footage hundreds of times: Aaron shrugging off the two teenagers who ran onto the field to congratulate him as he rounded second and headed toward third. Then, the great man headed for home and into history, mobbed at the plate by his teammates, then embraced by his parents.

It's one of the few blessed byproducts of the Barry Bonds home run mania-turned-steroid scandal that's gripped baseball for several years now: there is now a renewed appreciation—a more complete appreciation—for Henry Louis Aaron. Or in some instances, for much of the newest, youngest generation, Bonds' assault on baseball's home run hierarchy has almost served as an introduction: Kids, meet Hank Aaron—the game's greatest slugger, and yet so much more.

"People are always going to associate me with nothing but home runs. That's eventually what they'll do with Barry, too," Aaron said, before the release of *Game of Shadows*, the meticulously researched book that details Bonds' supposed steroid use. "But I like to think of myself as a totally complete ballplayer," Aaron said. "People say, 'Well, you hit 755 home runs.' Yes, but I was more than that."

"Mr. Henry Aaron, he could play," said Ralph Garr, the quicksilver, free-swinging Braves outfielder known as "The Roadrunner" when he played with Aaron from 1968-74. "Some

people can play injured and some people can't. That's what I liked about Henry: He could play, play hurt, and play smart.

"There's no way," Garr said, "to describe the greatness of Henry Aaron."

Let's try anyway. Yes, Aaron hit 755 homers (the last 22 in 1975 and '76, when he finished his career back in Milwaukee with the Brewers). Yet he only led the National League in home runs four times and never hit more than 47 homers in a season. Aaron holds more major-league batting records than any player in history. And always will. Even now, three decades after retiring, Aaron's accomplishments are absolutely mind-numbing. He remains the game's all-time leader in runs batted in (2,297), total bases (6,856), and extra-base hits (1,477). He won two National League batting titles, including a career-high .355 average in 1959 (when he also set personal bests of 223 hits and 400 total bases).

Aaron also won four Gold Gloves. In 1963, he became baseball's fifth 30-30 player with 44 homers and 31 steals. He stole 240 bases in his illustrious career while playing for predominantly power-laden teams. In '63, Aaron also led the league in homers, runs batted in (130), and total bases. With a dozen or so more hits, he might have won baseball's rare Triple Crown; he hit .319 to Tommy Davis' league-leading .326.

"I'm very proud of winning my Gold Gloves," said Aaron. "Also, my home runs. Batting titles. The [four] RBI titles. About the only thing I didn't do is win a stolen base title."

Aaron did all this despite never playing high school baseball. His high school didn't have a baseball team, so he played for a semi-pro team in his hometown, the Mobile Black Bears. In 1952, he was signed for $200 a month by the Indianapolis Clowns of the Negro League. The name was a misnomer. As Aaron once said, "We never made it to Indiana." Since the integration of major-league baseball had begun by then, and the Negro Leagues were not as competitive as they'd long been, the Indianapolis Clowns—which featured stars like King Tut and Spec Bebop—were more of a barnstorming outfit. Aaron played shortstop then and still batted cross-handed as a right-handed hitter: with his left hand above his right hand on the bat handle. A Boston

Braves scout named Dewey Griggs takes the honor of finally convincing
Aaron to hold the bat conventionally, with his left hand below his right.

The young Aaron learned much more in his brief Negro League
career than just how to properly hold a bat. On a weekend trip to
Washington, D.C., the Clowns' doubleheader at Griffith Stadium
(home of the Washington Senators) was rained out. As Aaron years
later told Lonnie Wheeler, who collaborated on Aaron's
autobiography, *I Had a Hammer*: "We had breakfast while we were
waiting for the rain to stop, and I can still envision sitting with the
Clowns in a restaurant behind Griffith Stadium and hearing [the
restaurant employees] break all the plates in the kitchen after we were
finished eating. What a horrible sound. Even as a kid, the irony of it
hit me: here we were in the capital in the land of freedom and equality,
and they had to destroy the plates that had touched the forks that had
been in the mouths of black men. If dogs had eaten off those plates,
they'd have washed them." This was an early, painful, lasting lesson of
the type of racism Aaron would encounter throughout most of his
baseball career—culminating, nearly a quarter-century later, with his
hate-filled countdown to breaking Babe Ruth's home run record.

Back in the Deep South, Dewey Griggs kept bird-dogging the
young Aaron. The kid failed a tryout with the Brooklyn Dodgers
because he was too skinny. Indeed, when Aaron arrived at his first
major-league spring training camp with the Braves in 1954,
equipment man Joe Taylor called out to manager Charlie Grimm,
"There's a skinny kid in the clubhouse carrying a duffel bag." Nearly
two years earlier, on May 25, 1952, having suggested the hitting hand-
switch to Aaron earlier that day, Griggs had written a letter to
Milwaukee general manager John Mullen that forecast the future.
"This boy could be the answer," Mullen signed off after giving a
scouting report on the gifted young stringbean.

In the kind of contractual move that alters history, Mullen paid
the Indianapolis Clowns $7,500 for Aaron and signed him to a Braves
contract for the princely salary of $350 a month. A second baseman,
Aaron starred in the club's farm system for two years; he was the
Northern League's Rookie of the Year while playing in Eau Claire,
Wisconsin, then the '53 Most Valuable Player of the South Atlantic

League with Jacksonville after leading the league in batting (.362) and RBIs (125). Struggling defensively as a second baseman, however, Aaron was converted to an outfielder while playing winter ball in Puerto Rico.

When his hero, the newly acquired Bobby "Shot Heard 'Round the World" Thomson, broke his ankle in St. Petersburg, Florida, during spring training in 1954, Aaron suddenly became the Braves' starting left fielder at age 20. In his first exhibition game in Thomson's stead, Aaron belted such a prodigious home run that Ted Williams ran out of the Boston clubhouse, wondering who'd hit a ball so hard to make such a sound. Teddy Ballgame always knew hitting, whether he saw it or merely heard it. Bobby Thomson knew, too.

"Magic is the only way to describe it," Thomson recalled the kid Aaron many years later. "You just had this feeling, even then, that this guy was something special. He was far removed from the ordinary class of ballplayer, like the rest of us.

"Some of the guys were skeptical. Everybody had said he was bound to be a great one. He'd hit well in the minors, sure, but we figured he'd be like so many other rookies: come to camp with a reputation, really see the curveball for the first time, and bomb out."

Aaron's ascendance to the major leagues coincided with the Braves' second season in baseball-happy Milwaukee. Despite finishing third, the club topped the two-million mark in attendance for the first time, drawing a record 2,131,388 fans that season. All of those paying customers got their first in-person look at the young Hank Aaron, who once matter-of-factly recalled his big-league debut: "My arrival in the major leagues was pretty dull. No drama, no excitement, absolutely none. I just arrived, that's all."

Not exactly. On Opening Day, Aaron went 0-for-5 in a 9-8 loss to the Cincinnati Reds. Ten days later, history commenced innocently enough. The rookie's first home run came in his seventh game, courtesy of Vic Raschi, the great Yankees right-hander who'd refused to take a cut in salary following the club's world championship season in 1953 and was traded to the St. Louis Cardinals. In Busch Stadium, Aaron took Raschi deep for the first of his 755 big-league homers.

"He had such great wrists," Raschi later recalled. "It was hard to fool him."

Milwaukee's highlight film following the 1954 season included precisely one shot of Henry Aaron. It showed the youngster hitting a foul ball. He did a bit more than that in '54, when Aaron finished second in the National League Rookie of the Year balloting to the Cardinals' Wally Moon. He batted .280 with 13 home runs and 69 runs batted in. Those numbers would've been higher had Aaron played a full season. By Labor Day weekend, Milwaukee was in the pennant race, just four games behind the Giants. On September 5, Aaron stroked five straight base hits in a doubleheader as the Braves swept Cincinnati. But on the fifth of those hits, a triple, Aaron broke his ankle sliding into third. Ironically, Bobby Thomson was the pinch runner called upon as Aaron was carried from the field to an ambulance. The Braves struggled to play .500 ball in Aaron's absence, and finished the season 89-65 and in third place, five games out. Aaron played 122 games that season; as a symbol of his durability, those 122 games were the fewest of his career until 1973, when he was 39 years old.

"Henry was very nice to people," said Garr. "If you came to him, you had all the help in the world. He'd say, 'The best way to keep your job is to do your job.' And, 'You can't help your club in the tub.' He used to tickle me."

In 1955, his second season in Milwaukee, Aaron blossomed. He made the NL All-Star team, the first of 21 straight appearances in the All-Star game—every time as a starter. It was also Aaron's first of 20 consecutive seasons with at least 20 home runs (he finished with 27), one of several trends he'd just begun. His first .300 season (.314) was one of 14 he'd manufacture; his 106 RBIs the first of 11 such seasons with 100-plus.

His 1956 campaign was yet another revelation. "Hammerin' Hank," as Donald Davidson, the Braves' diminutive traveling secretary and goodwill ambassador began calling Aaron (or simply "Hank," which Davidson felt was friendlier than "Henry"), demonstrated he was more than just a long-ball hitter. Much, much more. In addition to his 26 homers and 92 runs batted in, Aaron led the National League in batting with a .328 average, as well as hits (200), total bases (340), and doubles (34). In a twist, he also finished second in triples, with 14. Yet the Braves, in a torrid pennant race, finished a game behind Brooklyn with 92 wins.

"Throwing a fastball by Henry Aaron," Cardinals pitcher Curt Simmons said back then, "is like trying to sneak the sun past a rooster."

Yet it was the 1957 season in which Aaron awakened the nation to his all-around ability. He led the National League with 44 homers and 132 RBIs and batted .322 as the Braves won their first pennant in Milwaukee. Perhaps the most crucial of those 44 home runs came in late September against the fast-charging Cardinals, an 11th-inning, "walk-off" shot that clinched the pennant. As Aaron later remembered: "I galloped around the bases and when I touched home plate, the whole team was there to pick me up and carry me off the field. I had always dreamed about a moment like Bobby Thomson had in '51, and this was it."

Years later, Aaron acknowledged that the pennant-clinching homer—the 109th of his young career—was his most satisfying home run, more so than even his record-breaking 715th long ball. Aaron was voted the National League's MVP that season (for the first and only time in his career), and was one very prime reason why the Braves drew 2,215,404 fans, then the National League attendance record.

In the '57 World Series, Aaron sparkled and manager Fred Haney's Braves ultimately got revenge for the Yankees deriding Milwaukee as "bush." As he had during the regular season, Aaron's was a complete game in October, leading all players in the World Series in runs scored, base hits, home runs (three), batting average (.393), and runs batted in (seven). And when Lew Burdette beat New York for the third time in the Series with a 5-0 shutout in Game 7 in Yankee Stadium, the city of Milwaukee had its first World Series championship and a sense of vindication. Among thousands and thousands of delirious Braves fans celebrating downtown, one banner in particular fairly crowed, "Bushville Wins."

In 1958, Aaron won his first Gold Glove. But Milwaukee, which had stormed to leads of 2-0 and 3-1 in the World Series, lost in seven games to the Yankees. Aaron—spectacular once again that season with 30 homers, 95 RBIs, and a .326 average—batted .333 in the World Series but drove in just two runs.

It would never be the same for the Milwaukee Braves and Aaron, who would not see another postseason until franchise relocation and 11 seasons later. "I didn't realize it at the time," Aaron reflected years hence. "But after we won the seventh game of the World Series in 1957, everything started to go downhill."

In 1959, they lost to the Los Angeles Dodgers in a playoff for the NL pennant. Attendance dropped just below two million that year, and a steady decline began. Although the Braves continued to play winning baseball, they were no longer real contenders after finishing a distant second in 1960. By the mid-'60s, the Braves were far from the dominating team they had once been—although from 1959-63, Aaron hit at least 34 home runs in each season, including three 40-homer years. Crowds in County Stadium—once always teeming with baseball-mad Milwaukeeans—were significantly smaller. In 1965, the Braves barely topped a half-million in attendance. The novelty of big-league ball was long gone. By 1966, so were the Braves, Atlanta-bound.

"I'd heard whispers about the ballclub moving, but I didn't think it was for real," Aaron recalled from one of his Atlanta area car dealerships. "After we moved here, I realized the ballpark was going to be very friendly to me. That's the first thing a ballplayer looks at. I felt with my style of hitting, I could have a great career here.

"I had mixed emotions [about moving]," he said. "I was still young enough, I still had my career staring me in the face. I was really a young 30. My career had just begun. It wasn't like I was an old 30. I was just getting into my prime. I was ready to start blossoming."

The move to Atlanta altered far more than just Aaron's batting style. As he said in his autobiography, "Atlanta changed me as a hitter and a person at the same time. The real world made me angrier and hungrier than I had been as a young Milwaukee Brave. . . . I was tired of being invisible. I was the equal of any ballplayer in the world, damn it, and if nobody was going to give me my due, it was time to grab for it."

Before the Braves' first game in Atlanta, the 1966 season opener against Pittsburgh, Aaron had a premonition of what was to come: "Sometimes you play in a ballpark, and you can just feel no matter who's pitching or who you're playing, you can get a hit or hit the ball out of the park," he said. "In batting practice [before that Opening Night], I remember the ball was flying out in right, center, left.

"I thought if I stayed healthy," Aaron recalled, "I could do some things I couldn't have done if I'd stayed in Milwaukee."

Back up north in Wisconsin, Aaron typically hit the ball from right-center to left field. "When we moved here," he said, "I started pulling the ball more—center and left. I made myself into a pull hitter." He changed his stance somewhat, too. Instead of holding his bat as high, Aaron brought it in closer to his body. In Atlanta-Fulton County Stadium, which became known as "The Launching Pad" for the way the ball traveled, Aaron pulled the ball and placed himself in baseball's record book in the process.

In 1969, the Braves won the National League West Division and played in the first National League Championship Series, against the New York Mets. After an 11-year absence, Aaron was back in the postseason. It would be a cameo.

"I don't know if we were that good," Aaron said. "It was probably just a stroke of luck. We scored a lot of runs. We were not deep in pitching. And the Mets were very good."

Tom Seaver, Jerry Koosman, and the rest of the Miracle Mets swept the Braves. It would be Aaron's only postseason fling in Atlanta. A few seasons later, he was chasing the Babe, even if that was never the goal.

"I never thought about Babe Ruth, or catching him, or anybody else," Aaron said. "I thought, 'Just keep doing what you're doing.' There's a lot of things you can conquer if you do that."

Besides his remarkably strong, quick wrists, Aaron was a very intelligent hitter. An intuitive one, too: a guess hitter who could guess with the best of 'em and make a pitcher pay. As Dodger left-hander

Claude Osteen once said, "Slapping a rattlesnake across the face with the back of your hand is safer than trying to fool Henry Aaron."

By the time his pursuit of Ruth was in full force and very much in the public eye during the 1970 season, Aaron had become just the eighth player in baseball history to amass 3,000 hits. He was the very first to reach 3,000 hits and 500 home runs (just edging out Willie Mays for that distinction). In 1971, he'd hit a career-high 47 homers with a .327 average and 118 RBIs. That left Aaron with 673 home runs (41 shy of Ruth's record). It also earned him a new two-year contract, making Aaron the first player to earn a $200,000 annual salary.

In 1973, at the age of 39, he hit 40 homers, the most ever for a player that age. The Braves became the first team in major-league history with three 40-homer players, Aaron joining third baseman Darrell Evans (41) and second baseman Davey Johnson (43), who'd never hit more than 18 homers in a season in Baltimore but who erupted in his first year in Atlanta. Aaron finished the '73 season with 713 career home runs, one shy of the Babe. His final homer that year came in the penultimate game of the season, off Houston's Jerry Reuss on September 29. In the rainy season finale, Aaron faced Astros left-hander Dave Roberts, whom he'd hit No. 712 off the previous week in Houston's Astrodome.

Roberts had vowed not to give up another historic homer to The Hammer. "I don't want to be the one giving up the 714th or 715th home runs," Roberts said. "If he comes up in a situation with a chance to beat me, I'm going to pitch around him." Roberts' teammates were slightly less intense. They taped a note on the pitcher's locker. It read: "Thanks for Nos. 568, 599, 618, 655, 712, 714, and 715. Hank."

Roberts recalled, "They told me, 'You'll be famous, you'll make the banquet tour all winter. You can get fat serving up a fat pitch.'"

Roberts gave up three singles to Aaron in his first three at-bats. In his final at-bat of the season, in the eighth inning, Aaron faced fastballing Don Wilson, who jammed Aaron, broke his bat, and got him to pop out to third.

Afterward, Aaron even issued a personal apology to the nearly 41,000 fans who'd come out in hopes of seeing history. "I'm sorry I couldn't hit one for them, sitting in the rain like that," Aaron said following the game. "I was going for the home run. I wasn't trying to hit singles. And that applause, I guess, was the biggest moment I've had in baseball."

The season—an arduous, often unbearable journey that had become a hate-filled grind—was finally over. It was hardly a grand, joyous romp into baseball posterity. The closer Aaron came to Ruth, the more hate mail he received. It was racist, and vile, and sometimes life-threatening, invariably sent anonymously by white racists who didn't want him to break Ruth's record.

The City of Atlanta Police Department had assigned Aaron a bodyguard who traveled everywhere with him. A false rumor spread that Aaron's daughter had been kidnapped from her college dormitory. Aaron had to check into hotels under assumed names, sometimes even staying apart from his teammates at another hotel. Once Aaron had divulged his hate mail to sportswriters who'd tracked him much of the season, his mail subsequently turned more encouraging, less racist.

The U.S. postal system actually awarded Aaron a plaque at season's end. He'd received more mail than any non-politician in the country that year, over 930,000 letters. One letter from Texas, postmarked June 10, 1973, was addressed thusly: The word "The" was printed next to a photo of a hammer glued to an envelope, with "Atlanta Georgia" written in script beneath it. No problem: The letter was delivered to "The Hammer."

The ordeal, however, was hardly over. Not with Aaron still one home run shy of catching the Babe, two from supplanting him.

GAME OF MY LIFE

"All I've got to do this winter is stay alive."

That's what Hank Aaron said immediately after the 1973 season finale. It was a quiet, peaceful, joyful winter for him. Aaron got remarried, to Billye Williams. He also signed a long-term contract to endorse televisions and other products for the Magnavox Corporation.

It helped provide Aaron financial security, and his remarriage was a blessing. Still is.

The resumption of the Ruthian chase was blessedly brief. It was nowhere near as long, as arduous, as solitary as the '73 season had been. "My kids didn't enjoy it," Aaron recalled. "They were not with me. Nobody was with me. I was out on an island by myself. . . .

"I had to have a security guard with me, all the time," Aaron said. "He'd pick me up in the morning, take me to the game at night. I wasn't allowed to go here or there. I had no freedom."

No. 715 would prove liberating. Getting to that point, however, wasn't easy. The Braves opened the 1974 season on the road, in Cincinnati. Eager to finally get the damn thing over with, Aaron also wanted to do so in Atlanta.

"I live in Atlanta, and that's where I want to hit the home run that ties the record and the home run that breaks the record," he said before Opening Day. "I feel I owe it to the fans."

So Aaron stated that he wanted to play just the middle game of the three-game series in Cincinnati. Baseball commissioner Bowie Kuhn was not amused. He didn't want Aaron orchestrating the timetable for baseball history. He spoke to Bill Bartholomay, the Braves chairman of the board, and demanded the team play Aaron (who'd played 120 games in '73) in two of the three games in Riverfront Stadium. In his first at-bat of 1974, on his very first swing, Aaron jumped on a Jack Billingham fastball and belted it over the left-center-field wall to tie Ruth. He slowly circled the bases, then was enveloped by his jubilant teammates, waiting at home plate.

No. 715 would have to wait. In his next three at-bats that day, Aaron grounded out, drew a four-pitch walk, and lined out to center before being pulled in the seventh inning. Eddie Mathews, once the Braves' Hall of Fame slugging third baseman and Aaron's left-handed counterpart, was now the club's manager and fully intended to sit Aaron the rest of the weekend. An angry Kuhn ordered Mathews to start Aaron on Sunday. Mathews capitulated. Aaron struck out twice against the Reds' Clay Kirby before being pulled again in the seventh inning. On to Atlanta, and the home opener, April 8.

"Several things happened that night," Aaron recalled in his car dealership. "I felt particularly good about the fact that a friend I'd met several years earlier, Sammy Davis Jr., was there. And Maynard Jackson [later the mayor of Atlanta on two separate occasions], too. My father [Herbert] and mother [Estella] were there."

So were 53,775 fans, the largest crowd in Atlanta-Fulton County Stadium history. Ever the entertainer, Sammy Davis Jr. was also a smart, practical man; he offered Aaron $25,000 for the historic home run ball. The Hammer declined the offer. Aaron was the object of a 45-minute pregame salute. National TV networks were there, primed and ready. Chief Noc-a-Homa, a Chippewa Indian named Levi Walker who played the Braves mascot and had a teepee in the left-field stands, brought a lacrosse stick to the stadium, hoping to snare the 715th ball.

In his first at-bat that evening, Aaron didn't even swing at a pitch. Al Downing, the Dodgers' veteran left-hander, walked him on five pitches. In the fourth inning, with L.A. leading 3-1, Darrell Evans was on first base when Downing missed low with his first pitch to Aaron. The next pitch, at 9:07 p.m., was a fastball—a fat fastball. Aaron crushed it toward left-center field. Jimmy Wynn, the Dodgers' center fielder, and left fielder Bill Buckner converged near the wall. Neither leapt for the ball. Not that it mattered; the ball sailed over the wall. "We kind of wanted Aaron to get it over with," Buckner said afterward, "so he could go back to being a human being."

As Aaron ran toward first, he spied Jim Busby, the Braves first base coach, jumping for joy. At that moment, he knew that he'd done it. Dodgers' second baseman Davey Lopes, then shortstop Bill Russell, both shook Aaron's hand as he jogged around the bases. The stadium shook. And the ball? It landed in the Braves bullpen, smack in the glove of reliever Tom House. Teammate Jamie Easterly tried to catch it, but ran into a cannon situated behind the fence and in front of the left-field stands.

For House, standing some 350 feet from the plate, watching the 715 ball zoom toward him "blew my mind." He recalled: "The ball was rising on a line. If I'd frozen like a dummy, the ball would've hit me in the forehead. The only problem, though, was a guy above me who had a fishnet on a pole. He couldn't get it operating in time."

Aaron couldn't get to home plate quickly enough for his teammates. They mobbed him, ecstatically. A chilly and damp night was suddenly something bright and beautiful. House, having run in from the bullpen with the rest of the relievers, hand-delivered the ball to Aaron. There was a brief on-field ceremony. Once the game resumed and Aaron next came to bat, the ballpark was nearly empty. They'd witnessed what they'd come to see.

In the clubhouse afterward, a congratulatory phone call came through from beleaguered United States President Richard Nixon. Aaron hoisted a glass of champagne. To a swarm of reporters, he pronounced a weight that felt like "a stove" was lifted off his back. "To be honest, all I wanted to do was touch the bases," Aaron then said softly. "Other than that, I don't really remember the noise, or the two kids on the field. My teammates at the plate, I do remember seeing them. I remember my mother out there, and her hugging me.

"That's what I remember more than anything when I think back on it," he said. "I don't know where she came from, but she was there. I feel I can relax now. I feel my teammates can relax."

In retrospect, what particularly pleased Aaron was the location—not just of Downing's fastball, but, a la his one-time hero and teammate, Bobby Thomson, his very own shot heard 'round the world."

"It was the fact that I did it, and in the ballpark in Atlanta," Aaron now says. "Despite all the controversy that was part of it, I did it in Atlanta."

It was a tremendous relief. "Oh, God, yes it was," Aaron said. "People don't realize what a relief it was. I had been to hell and back, twice. It was so hard. It was pitiful the way it panned out. Wherever I went—New York, Chicago, wherever—there was always something in the paper about 'Babe Ruth and Henry.' I got tons of letters, hateful and spiteful.

"I was glad it was done and over with," Aaron said. "Now, I could get on with my life. People don't realize how I almost had a nervous breakdown. It was really downright horrible, a terrible year and a half."

✳ ✳ ✳

Aaron would hit 18 more homers that season, his 20th consecutive season with at least 20 home runs. That winter, at the age of 40, Aaron was traded to Milwaukee, where he'd begun his career and would end it two seasons later.

"The greatest thing that ever happened to me," Aaron said of the trade. "In spring training, we were in a little resort town in Arizona. That was serene. Nobody bothered me."

He played his last major-league game on October 3, 1976. A crowd of 6,858 watched. Aaron felt it was "embarrassing" to conclude his career with a season in which he batted .229. He's the only person who felt that way.

After retiring, Aaron returned to Atlanta and the Braves, for whom he served 13 years as a vice president and director of player development. "But I knew I wouldn't stay in baseball all of my life," Aaron said. "I started making the transition to business."

After some bad early investments, business and life have become very good for Hank Aaron. He's become extremely business savvy, and completely involved in his business interests.

"I approach business the way I approached baseball: I work very hard," Aaron said. "I've met some very nice people and have been helped by some people around me. I'm very thankful."

The BMW dealership was one of six auto dealerships of which Aaron was the majority owner before selling his share in five of them; his 755 Restaurant Corp. owns nearly two dozen fast-food outlets in Georgia and the Carolinas, including Church's Chicken and Krispy Kreme franchises. When Aaron turned 70 on February 5, 2004, 150 of his family, friends, and associates gathered to celebrate the occasion.

These days, Hank Aaron is a multimillionaire who's reveling in the Braves' success and his own good fortune. "It is gratifying," Aaron said of the Braves' unexpected run to an unprecedented 14 straight division titles. "Despite all the salaries and all these other things that put baseball in a different light now, the ballclub kept winning. People attribute a lot of it to Bobby Cox, and you have to. People say John Schuerholz, too. That's true, but it's mostly the manager. Bobby has worked through high payrolls, low payrolls, and minimum payrolls, and he's won championships with them. You'd have to say almost 80 percent of it is him."

And as for himself, life now as a septuagenarian is very, very good for Hank Aaron, the all-time home run king and the man whose name graces the awards given to the top hitters in each league each season.

"I feel good," Aaron said. "I'm here. My kids are here. I've got grandkids I'm very proud of. I'm happy with myself."

As he should be—he deserves it.

Chapter 14

GENE GARBER

s job changes go, Gene Garber's was slightly traumatic. You could say that. Just as you could say that water is wet and that Garber was having a bad day in June of 1978. You would have been, too, if you'd just been traded from the front-running Philadelphia Phillies to the bad news Braves of Atlanta.

"I was leaving a first-place club, the Phillies," Garber said. "We'd won the NL East Division in '76 and '77, and were well on the way to winning in '78. But we needed starting pitching. So I was the one who got traded to Atlanta."

Garber recounts this 28 years and several hundred miles removed from Atlanta, from his Lancaster County, Pennsylvania, farm that he now runs with his two sons. There in eastern Pennsylvania, on nearly 400 acres, Garber, 59, operates a successful farm with egg-layer chickens and grows crops of corn, soy beans, wheat, barley, and hay. Garber still raises some emus, too, the ostrich-like animals who provide meat, eggs, and oil that is used as an anti-inflammatory to treat sore muscles and joints. The former closer with 19 years on his big-league resume needs no such relief, however, and the anxiety and pain from that long-ago trade has long since subsided.

The day before his trade, the Phillies had picked up reliever Rawly Eastwick, causing the already-full Philly bullpen to bulge at the seams. Manager Danny Ozark called a meeting of his pen, including Tug McGraw, Ron Reed, and Garber, all short relievers. "Danny said, 'Don't worry, we're not trading any of you guys. We just got the opportunity to pick up Rawly Eastwick,'" Garber recalled. "When we left the meeting and looked at each other, we all said, 'Okay, who's it gonna be?'"

After coming from Kansas City to Philadelphia in 1974, Garber had carved out a nice niche in the Phillies bullpen. In '75, he'd led the National League in appearances with 71. He then helped the Phils win consecutive NL East titles, going 9-3 with a 2.82 earned-run average and 11 saves in '76, then registering 19 saves in '77.

"I grew up 90 miles from Philadelphia," said Garber, now back in his hometown of Elizabethtown. "I grew up a Phillies fan. It was just great. And then to be traded, and to a club that was a perennial loser, it was tough to take."

The weekend before the trade, Philadelphia had a three-game series in San Diego. "We got into the hotel that Thursday about 7 or 8 at night," Garber said. "By some quirk, there was not a key for me at the front desk. I saw Danny Ozark and [pitching coach] Ray Rippelmeyer were talking off to the side of the lobby. Joking, I said, 'Okay, where have I been traded?'

"Then I saw the look on their faces," Garber said. "I knew I'd been traded. Danny said, 'Well, can we talk?'"

Destination: Last-place Atlanta. "I couldn't believe it," Garber said. "I got traded for Dick Ruthven. I knew Dick, he'd been with the Phillies, and they needed starting pitching. But still . . ."

Atlanta? What's a first-place guy to do?

"I give Bill Lucas a lot of credit for this," Garber said of the then-Braves' general manager—the first African-American to hold that position in the major leagues. "I found out the Braves were coming out to play San Diego the following Tuesday. Later that evening, Bill Lucas called and said, 'We have a flight for you, tomorrow evening. You can fly back to Atlanta.'"

Garber knew the Braves, who were home that weekend, were then flying west to play on the West Coast. Also, he was still stunned and angry about the trade. Having just flown cross-country to San Diego, why fly back east to Atlanta for a few days, then turn around and fly back to California?

"I said to Bill, 'This is a real shock for me. A very traumatic time,'" Garber said. "I told him, 'I'd like, if I could, to fly my wife out to San Diego, and take this weekend, take three days to mentally accept this trade from a first-place club to a last-place club. And I will do everything I can to be ready to play.'

"Bill said, 'Gene, that's a great idea.' By the time the Braves got into town Monday night, I'd accepted that trade and was in a much better frame of mind. I felt that made all the difference in the world to me, having those three days to come to grips with it. Not that I was a star, but it was traumatic."

Life in Atlanta initially wasn't much better. "It was pretty futile down there for quite a few years," Garber said. "In '78, Bill was bringing a lot of new guys in. [Dale] Murphy was young. [Bob] Horner was a No. 1 draft choice. He called up Hubby [second baseman Glenn Hubbard]. Called [catcher Bruce] Benedict up, too. But there were a lot of growing pains."

There was, however, one shining moment in that otherwise dismal, 69-93 washout in '78: The night of August 1, in Atlanta-Fulton County Stadium, Gene Garber got his piece of hardball history. "You can't ask for anything more than to pitch in meaningful games," Garber said. Less than two months after being traded to Atlanta, Garber had a most meaningful game, and foe: Pete Rose and his National League-record 44-game hitting streak.

"I told my wife when the Reds came into town, 'You know what, Karen? I feel I'm going to be the one to stop the streak. If Pete doesn't have a hit, we'll probably have the lead and I'd be pitching,'" recalled Garber, by then fully established as Atlanta's closer.

The Reds' Big Red Machine, which had won consecutive World Series in 1975-76, was still largely intact. That was apparent the previous evening, when the Reds won in a rout.

"They slaughtered us bad," Garber said. "They beat us big and were pretty much standing in the dugout, laughing at us. The next night, though, we were up 6-4. I faced Pete in the seventh inning. He hit a line shot right at Horner for an out.

"In the bottom of the seventh, we scored some runs, and in the eighth a ton. We led 16-4. Even I scored a run. Bobby [Cox] comes up to me and says, 'Gene, I'm gonna take you out.' I said, 'No, you can't. Bobby, I'm gonna end this streak.' He still wanted to take me out and I said, 'Bobby, I will start and go nine for you tomorrow night, but I'm staying in.'

"He looked at me, and said, 'Go get 'em, Geno.' That's one of the reasons guys love playing for Bobby Cox. We're not playing for first place. If we win, we're still 10 games out of fifth place. But we're gonna play hard for him.

"In the ninth inning, I think I struck the first two guys out. I knew Pete was the third batter. There's two outs, [the score is] 16-4, and all of a sudden I think, 'If I walk him here, I'll be as low as you can get! I'll never live it down.' For the only time in my life, I was scared I was going to walk somebody.

"I got behind him 2-1. I said, 'Man oh man, I can't walk him.' I thought, 'I have to throw him my changeup—my best pitch. My changeup was a feel pitch. I could feel when it left my hand if it was a good pitch or not.

"When I released it, it felt good. Pete fouled it off. I said, 'Man, that was a good pitch. How'd he foul it off?' I threw a change again. I said, 'Oh, no!' It came right down the middle, screaming, 'Hit me! Hit me! Hit me!' And Pete swung right through it [and struck out].

"They had an interview room set up afterward. Now in Atlanta in 1978, they didn't need a postgame interview room, but they had one set up anyway. I grabbed a Coke and went into our lounge: 'Okay, what am I gonna say?' I see Pete on the TV, live.

"He said, 'I can't believe, with a 16-4 lead, Garber's pitching to me like it's the ninth inning of the World Series.' I said, 'Thank you, Pete. That's the best compliment I'll ever get.' Knucksie [Phil Niekro] always said, 'Make each pitch like it's the last one of your career.' That's the way I approached my career.

"Pete kept talking. I never did go into the interview room. But I stayed in the clubhouse and answered question after question for all these reporters. When they asked about what Pete had said about pitching like it's the ninth inning of the World Series, I said, 'I have a feeling that's exactly the way Pete hit for, what, 14,000 at-bats? That's why he was probably the best hitter in the game."

Larry McWilliams, a rookie and Atlanta's starting pitcher that night, did appear for the postgame interview. In fact, he sat next to Rose at one point. Early in the game, McWilliams made a terrific one-handed stop of a blast off Rose's bat to deny him a single. Gary Caruso, then covering the game for the *Atlanta Journal*, recalled that afterward, when McWilliams was sitting beside Rose, Charlie Hustle had no idea who the kid was.

Rose knew Garber, however. The next night, after singling four times, he was still carping that Garber had pitched him so carefully and craftily the previous evening, working the corners instead of coming right at him. "I honestly think," Rose said that August 2, "that in that last at-bat, Garber didn't throw me a single strike."

"To this day, just about every anniversary that comes around, I get a call from somebody somewhere in the country who wants to write a story about it," said Garber.

✳ ✳ ✳

In 1979, Garber suffered 16 losses with the moribund Braves, then a big-league record for a reliever. Yet he also was third in the NL with 25 saves.

"There were a lot of growing pains," Garber said of the Braves of that era. "It still took a lot of changes for that team to be brought up to where it was in '82.

"One of the things I think that really set that organization back was Bill Lucas' death [of an aneurysm in May, 1979, following a massive cerebral hemorrhage at his home]. He'd been doing a lot of good things. He was a great man, a man of integrity, and the players really liked him. He was very similar to Paul Owens [Garber's GM in Philadelphia]. What they said, you could take it to the bank."

After he struggled through difficult seasons in 1980 and '81, Garber and the Braves took off in '82 under new manager Joe Torre, who'd replaced Bobby Cox. "I remember starting the season 13-0," Garber said, laughing, "and then struggling later on." After an NL-record 13 straight wins to open the season and later opening up a 10-game lead on the Dodgers, the Braves would lose 11 in a row and 19 of 21 games by mid-August to plummet out of first place.

"Now, after watching baseball for 18 years [in retirement], watching ESPN and Fox Sports, they talk about how you get into September and a four-game lead is insurmountable," Garber said. "That's not true. And just the opposite, too: if you're four games up, you lose [the lead] in four days, even if you're not playing the other [second-place] team.

"One of the keys," he said, "is to realize that when things are going bad, the team is not as bad as it appears. And when it's really going good, the team's not that good."

After another miraculous run—winning six consecutive games, nine of 10, and 13 of 15—the Braves reclaimed first place. Yet they fell behind Los Angeles again, trailing by three games with 10 to play before a five-game Dodger losing streak—and Atlanta's split of a two-game series in Chavez Ravine in the last week of the season—gave the Braves a one-game lead entering the final weekend. When it was over, when Atlanta had prevailed and somehow won the West, Garber found himself sitting in the clubhouse in San Diego, sitting with Phil Niekro, who'd waited 13 long years to return to the postseason.

"I remember sitting back in the training room with Knucksie," Garber said. "He'd played all those years in Atlanta after the '69 playoffs, and now he's finally getting to do it again. He'd just come through a Hall of Fame outing [beating San Diego in that final Friday night] just to get us there. It didn't matter that he's 40 years old. He's a Hall of Famer.

"I remember we sat in that San Diego clubhouse," Gaber recalled. "He's had 13 years of futility in Atlanta. I didn't have but five. It wasn't as long as him, but we just sat there and savored it."

In the NLCS against St. Louis, "the weather really killed us," Garber said. "We flew right to St. Louis from San Diego. When we finally got back home to Atlanta [for Game 3], we'd been gone for two weeks.

"For six of those days, we'd been water-logged in St. Louis," said Garber. "We felt the game they called in St. Louis [Game 1, with Niekro up 1-0 and two out in the fifth inning when a rain delay turned into a postponement], they took that one from us. It didn't rain any harder [once play was halted]. There was no reason for that game to be called with two outs in the fifth. That situation was uncalled for."

The Cardinals swept the Braves in three games. Torre felt Garber—and his 30 saves—had been so valuable, that he pushed his player for NL MVP consideration. Garber finished seventh in the NL Cy Young voting, and Atlanta's bullpen was named the National League's best.

In '83, however, Garber was hampered by a sore pitching elbow and lost his job as the club's go-to closer. He pitched two seasons of middle relief before resuming his closer's role in '86 and registering 24 saves. But then he was traded to Kansas City in 1987, retired after the '88 season, and went home to Pennsylvania to farm.

With his characteristic side-winding delivery and lethal changeup, Garber made 922 relief appearances (931 games overall). Of his 218 saves, 141 came in Atlanta, a Braves record that stood until John Smoltz broke it in 2004.

GAME OF MY LIFE

"The Rose game is what I'm known for, and remembered for. But the game of my life was the year before I got traded from Philadelphia. We're playing the Dodgers in the 1977 NLCS.

"We were tied 1-1 in a best-of-five. I come in, it's a 3-3 game in the seventh inning. We get two runs in the bottom of the eighth and we've got a 5-3 lead. I'd faced eight guys, and got eight guys out—three in the seventh, three in the eighth, and the first two in the ninth.

"With two outs in the ninth inning, I've got an 0-2 count on Vic Davalillo. And he dragged a bunt between first and second. I couldn't get to the ball. He couldn't have rolled it any better. The next hitter was Manny Mota. He hit a fly ball to left field.

"It was really windy. Greg Luzinski was our left fielder. There were about five things we did in that inning that we never [typically] did. Jerry Martin would usually come in for Luzinski for defensive purposes. But Bull [Luzinski], if he got his glove on it, he'd catch it. But he drifted a little with Mota's ball. It was windy. Bull got back to the fence and reached up and the ball hit off his glove. Then it hit off the wall, and he got it and threw to second base. The ball hit a seam in the turf and bounced bad, and it bounced away from Ted Sizemore at second. They gave the error to Sizemore, and an assist to Luzinski.

"So Mota goes to third. Davey Lopes hits a hard ground ball to [third baseman Mike] Schmidt, just to his left. It rolled toward [Larry] Bowa at short, who barehanded the ball and threw to first. The throw just beat Lopes. But Bruce Froemming was the first base umpire, and he called Lopes safe. Richie Hebner was at first for us, and he was so sure Lopes was out, he took his cap and drop-kicked it to Froemming.

"[During the next at-bat] I threw over to first base. I knew Lopes was going to steal. One of my throws hit Lopes—I'm not sure how— and it went over into foul territory and he went to second. Billy Russell then hit a ground ball right back between my legs and Lopes scored.

"There were 62,000 people in the Vet. Actually. . ." Garber paused and checked the box score of that game. "63,719 people in the Vet, and they'd been chanting, 'Gee-NO! Gee-NO!' And I couldn't have pitched any better. Eight up, eight down. I had a two-strike count and a guy bunts, and all of a sudden the roof caved in.

"I spent probably an hour that night defending Bruce Froemming, saying, 'Hey, he wasn't trying to miss that call.' He saw it as being safe; we all saw it as being out. I know I didn't sleep one minute that night.

"We had Carlton pitching the next night. Steve pitched eight innings but we end up losing 4-1. To [manager] Danny Ozark's credit, he got me back in there in the ninth that night. It rained hard all night, and we lost the series 3-1.

"All the starch was taken out of our sails the night before. If we'd won, I'm confident we would've won the series. I had such fun pitching that night. But then it ended up being a total nightmare."

Chapter 15

RALPH GARR

Ralph Garr? In a word . . .

"Beep-beep!"

As in *The Roadrunner*, the animated cartoon character with blazing speed who made but one sound: "Beep-beep!" That became Ralph Garr's nickname, "The Roadrunner," when he jumped from Triple-A Richmond to Atlanta for good in 1971.

"'The Roadrunner' was a copyrighted name," said Garr. "In Richmond, I stole 60-something bases. When I came to the Braves, Mr. Bob Hope asked Warner Brothers if he could use the name."

Hope, then the Braves' public relations maven and promotional wizard, got permission from the studio and hyped Garr as "The Roadrunner." Yet it wasn't just his speed on the basepaths or chipper persona that made Garr one of the most popular Braves of the '70s. It was his bat. The sweet combination of contact hitter-meets-sprinter was lethal.

"I've always been able to hit a little bit," Garr said, "wherever I was. I won batting titles in the Dominican Republic, too, in 1969 and '70 when I played winter ball there. I hit .400 one year."

Yet Garr made his major-league mark in Atlanta. After brief call-ups by the Braves in 1968-70, Garr arrived for good in '71 and scorched the National League. A free-swinging outfielder who rarely met a pitch he didn't like, Garr batted .343 and collected 219 hits. Both of those marks were second in the NL to Joe Torre, the former Brave who was voted the National League's Most Valuable Player that season with St. Louis.

"Joe Torre hit .363 that year and I was sort of overlooked," said Garr, who set a club record (that still stands) with 219 hits that season. Due to the 70 Braves games he appeared in during the three previous seasons, Garr was ineligible for Rookie of the Year honors in '71. No matter. He set the tone for five spectacular offensive seasons in Atlanta.

"I made contact," said Garr, who hit a composite .317 for the Braves, still an Atlanta record. "I used a big bat [36 inches long, with a weight of 38 ounces] and I just used my speed."

Batting leadoff mostly, but occasionally hitting second, Garr got his licks in. "I wasn't a guy who took a lot of pitches," he said. "I was aggressive, really aggressive. I attacked the ball all the time. You could fool me, but I was a pretty good fastball hitter. I didn't care how hard you threw.

"Some guys could trick me and keep me off stride," Garr said. "I was just blessed with instinct. I just tried to put the ball in play."

A left-handed hitter, Garr was born in Monroe, Louisiana. He played collegiately at Grambling and led the NAIA with a .568 batting average in 1967. By then, his unique batting style and approach to hitting was well established. "I'd pull away from the plate," Garr said. "I'd swing running. If I used a big bat, I could cover the outside part of the plate."

In a lineup of even bigger bats, Ralph Garr was the eternal table-setter. "We had a young man named Mr. Henry Aaron," he said. "We were no Punch 'n' Judy club. We were hitters.

"With Henry batting third, he could drive you in from first," Garr said. "We had Darrell Evans, Earl Williams, Davey Johnson, later Dusty Baker."

"The Roadrunner" had a clear, well-defined role: Get on base, then get home any way possible. Garr led Atlanta in hits each year

from 1971-75, including three 200-hit seasons. He led the National League in hits in '74 with 214. He also led the ballclub in stolen bases from 1971-75, with a career-high 35 in '73. His greatest season came in 1974, when Garr made the NL All-Star team and led the league in hitting with a career-high .353 average—fully 32 percentage points ahead of the runnerup, Pittsburgh's Al Oliver. His 214 hits included 17 triples, most in the National League and still an Atlanta record. His slugging percentage was a robust .503.

"In 1974, everything went well," Garr said of his lone All-Star campaign. He credits his success to a steady diet of fastballs down the middle of the plate, as opposing pitchers worried about Aaron breaking the home run record. Aaron did just that on April 8, 1974. Ironically, up until that point—just four games into the season—Garr was 0-for-16 at the plate. Once Aaron had passed Ruth, Garr went on a tear: 25-for-48. An 0-for-5 night broke his modest 11-game hitting streak, but Garr started another the next day, a 12-game streak. All told, after that initial 0-for-16 slump—his longest of the season—Garr would go hitless in just four more contests during the first two months of the season; 12 times he would collect three or more hits in a game over that same stretch. The hot streak propelled Garr to new heights, as he became the first player since 1930 to amass 200 hits by the end of August. Garr posted 64 multi-hit games that year; the only thing that could stop him was an injury, which kept him out of the lineup for nearly three weeks in September.

In 1975, however, Garr's average fell to .278 as the Braves likewise tumbled to 67-94. In December of '75, under new Braves owner Ted Turner, Garr was traded to the Chicago White Sox for outfielder Ken Henderson and pitcher Dick Ruthven. He spent four seasons on the South Side of Chicago before finishing his career with the California Angels in 1980. A lifetime .306 hitter, Garr was baseball's No. 2 hitter in the 1970s. His .314 batting average during the decade of disco was surpassed only by eventual Hall of Famer Rod Carew.

"I had a wonderful time in Chicago, but I've always been a Brave in my heart," said Garr. A Braves scout since 1985, he now lives in Houston and is the scouting department's area supervisor for southeast Texas.

"I went with the organization when you could throw a ball in the stands and not hit [a person]," Garr said of times when attendance was markedly low. "Now, you can barely get in the place.

"It was a blessing to come from a small college and go to the Braves and win a batting title," he said. "The Braves have just been my life. I've really been blessed."

Those blessings multiplied on August 11, 2006, when Garr was inducted into the Braves Hall of Fame. It was an especially meaningful and emotional day for Garr, who was joined in the Hall's eighth class by the late Bill Lucas. A one-time Braves farmhand whose career was ended by a knee injury in 1964, Lucas became the public relations director for the minor-league Atlanta Crackers in 1965. He was part of the transition team that facilitated the Braves' move from Milwaukee to Atlanta; then Lucas worked his way up through the club's organization: In 1967, as the assistant farm director, later the farm director; and finally, in 1976, as baseball's first African-American general manager. Lucas died suddenly in 1979 at the age of 43.

"They inducted me and Mr. Bill Lucas," Garr said. "That meant a lot to me. Well, it's just a good thing when someone thinks enough of you to induct you into their hall of fame."

That day, Garr and Lucas (who was represented by his widow, Rubye) became the 18th and 19th inductees into the Braves Hall of Fame. They joined their predecessors Hank Aaron, Bill Bartholomay, Lew Burdette, Skip Caray, Del Crandall, Tommy Holmes, Ernie Johnson, Herman Long, Eddie Mathews, Dale Murphy, Kid Nichols, Phil Niekro, Johnny Sain, Paul Snyder, Warren Spahn, Ted Turner, and Pete Van Wieren.

On that happy Friday afternoon, during the Hall of Fame luncheon and ceremony in the 755 Club at Turner Field, something was missing for Ralph Garr: his wife, Ruby, who was ill and couldn't make the trip from Houston to Atlanta. "She was diagnosed with breast cancer," Garr said a couple of months later. "She's doing pretty good now."

That Friday, Garr missed his wife terribly. "I'm not crying tears of sadness," he tearfully told the luncheon audience. "They're all of joy, because I've been blessed. But to have a wife that has been with me 38 years and then to come here and be inducted into the Hall of Fame in Atlanta, and she's not able to be here, it makes you feel a little off. But she knows I love her."

The induction luncheon had its lighter moments, however. Niekro, who played with Garr in Atlanta, recalled his teammate's singular batting style. "My brother Joe used to ask me, 'How do you get Ralph Garr out?'" Niekro said. "I told him, 'I don't know.' Ralph's strike zone was between the two white lines." The foul lines.

When he composed himself again that day, Garr—who was recently honored with the Buck O'Neil Professional Scouts and Coaches Association Man of the Year Award—said, "When you're inducted into a hall of fame, that's a wonderful thing. People think you've done enough good things to contribute to the sports that you should be rewarded for what you've done.

"It's a pleasure," said The Roadrunner, "to be a part of the Braves organization."

GAME OF MY LIFE

"I remember one game in Atlanta, it was against the Mets. I hit a couple of home runs in Fulton County Stadium. I hit a homer off Tom Seaver, in the eighth or the ninth inning, to tie the game. And then I hit one in the 13th inning off Ron Taylor to win it. That was just something that [made me proud].

"I didn't have many multi-homer games [Garr hit just 49 total home runs in his six full seasons in Atlanta]. I was mostly a line-drive singles hitter. And I hadn't had a whole lot of success against Seaver. He was *unreal*. . . . That's why that game just stands out: I got a chance to have a pretty good day against one of the best pitchers in baseball.

"There were so many good pitchers then, and all of 'em were pretty tough for me: Bob Gibson, Seaver, Larry Dierker, Steve Carlton, Jerry Reuss, Don Wilson, J.R. Richard. Seaver was very tough. He didn't give up too many homers. In fact, that was the first time I ever hit a home run off him."

But it wouldn't be his last. While Garr only hit .245 against Seaver in his career, he did take him deep twice. Not too shabby for a guy who made a name for himself as one of the game's elite leadoff hitters of the '70s.

Chapter 16

TERRY PENDLETON

It would become, in Stan Kasten's words, "the greatest free-agent signing in history." Yet in December of 1990, when the abysmal Atlanta Braves signed Terry Pendleton to a four-year, $10.6 million contract, the St. Louis Cardinals third baseman was a stumpy 29-year-old coming off his worst season, and offering little promise of the miracles soon to come.

Only one other team—the New York Yankees—was interested in Pendleton, who'd hit just .230 in his Cardinal farewell, with but six homers and 58 RBIs. Although the Yankees offered more money, Pendleton accepted the Braves' four-year, $10.6 million offer, in large part because he felt his family would enjoy living in Atlanta more than New York.

"I knew the Braves had a lot of good young pitchers," he said. "John Schuerholz and Bobby Cox assured me they wanted to tighten up the infield. They felt like they had some good young pitchers and they just needed someone to catch the ball behind them."

Still, it wasn't like Pendleton was in big demand.

"Here's a guy who St. Louis was throwing away," recalled Mark Lemke, then a backup second baseman and a revelation-in-waiting himself. "Todd Zeile was playing third base for them. And I'm thinking, 'We're signing him for four years? What are we doing?'

"But my uncle living in St. Louis said, 'You've gotta see him every day. You're gonna love Pendleton.'"

Smart guy, Lemke's uncle. By May of '91, it was evident why Schuerholz, the Braves' new general manager, coveted Pendleton: for his Gold Glove defense behind Atlanta's "Young Guns" rotation; for his bat, resuscitated in the "Launching Pad" that was Atlanta-Fulton County Stadium; and for his leadership and professionalism. By that fall, all of Atlanta loved Pendleton as well as each of his teammates.

"I'd have to put '91 at the top, as my most satisfying season," Pendleton said, "and not because of my accolades." Pendleton won the National League batting title, hitting .319 with 22 home runs and 86 RBIs. "The anchor of our team," Schuerholz called the switch-hitter who was the first Brave to lead the league in both average and hits (187) since Ralph Garr in 1974. Pendleton was named the NL's Most Valuable Player and its Comeback Player of the Year. In leading Atlanta to an almost inconceivable pennant, he helped restore dignity to a long-maligned franchise; foster a rare love affair between a team and its city, state and region; and prompt an unprecedented run of excellence.

"I got the opportunity to watch young men grow into men and develop into damn good ballplayers," Pendleton said. "I saw young kids walk out on the field with their chests caved in to start the season, and at the end of the year, they're walking around on everybody's field like they owned the place.

"I got to meet people, fans from different states—Georgia, Alabama, Florida, South Carolina, North Carolina, Mississippi—who didn't know each other, who came to Atlanta-Fulton County Stadium and became one as a people," said Pendleton, a native Californian. "It didn't matter whether they were black, white, green, orange. It had nothing to do with race or color. It had to do with that little white ball out there, and the guy with the tomahawk on his shirt."

In a distinguished 15-year career (a .270 lifetime average, runner-up for the '92 National League MVP, three Gold Gloves, six division

titles, five World Series, and untold admiration from teammates and opponents alike), Pendleton was a prime protagonist when the "Tomahawk Chop" was born and the Braves set about winning. And winning. And winning, and . . .

"Terry is probably the greatest baseball player I've ever played with," Lemke says now. "I always tell Chipper [Jones] he's the most talented player I ever played with. But on and off the field, in the clubhouse, as a mentor, a leader, Terry's the greatest.

"If I'm managing," said the Lemmer, "I've gotta have him on my team."

"Bobby Cox and John Schuerholz told me, 'We feel like you have the qualities to lead this ballclub," Pendleton said. "I told them, 'I lead by example, bust my tail, and play hard. But I will speak up if something needs to be said.'"

When the Braves, a surprising three games out of first place in late June, lost three of four to Los Angeles in Atlanta and then two of three in Chavez Ravine to fall 9½ games back at the All-Star break, Lemke remembers Pendleton pacing in the visitors dugout in Dodger Stadium, repeating, "This isn't over. This isn't over."

On the flight home, Pendleton said, "Guys were walking up and down the aisle saying, 'Hey, we haven't even started to play yet and we're only 9½ games back.' I'm grinning. I'm enjoying this: 'Okay, now they have an idea of what's necessary.'"

When the Braves won seven of eight games to start the second half, and the Dodgers dropped seven of eight, the divisional race was on. The hysteria was on full throttle, too.

"I'd go into a store and it was almost like [I was] the second coming of God," Pendleton said. "I remember getting into the batter's box one night after Sid Bream hit a grand slam. I had to step out.

"I couldn't think; my concentration's gone," Pendleton recalled. "My ears were just ringing from the crowd noise, and I wore a double-flapped helmet."

"He showed the rest of the team how to act in a pennant race," said Jeff Treadway, the starting second baseman that season until a September injury. Pendleton hit .353 in his last 28 games. His solo homer on September 11 beat San Diego 1-0 as Kent Mercker, Mark

Wohlers, and Alejandro Pena combined on a no-hitter. One month later, Pendleton was back in his veteran's role as his team battled the Pirates in the NLCS. "I always try to take the pressure off the young kids, with the press, the media," he said. He recalls when the Braves' flight landed in Pittsburgh and the team buses headed toward downtown: "On the right side of the interstate was a big 20-by-20-foot sign, all lit up: 'The Night the Lights Went Out in Georgia!'

"I hollered to the boys on the bus, 'Look what they think of you guys!' They said, 'We'll see.'"

In the clubhouse before Game 6 of the NLCS the following night, with Atlanta trailing 3-2, "I told the boys the same speech Ozzie Smith gave us in St. Louis before Game 6 with San Francisco [in 1987]," Pendleton said. "I said, 'Fellas, if you win Game 6, Game 7 will be a cakewalk.'"

Behind Steve Avery, Atlanta won a suspenseful 1-0 nail-biter, just as St. Louis had in '87. In Game 7, Brian Hunter's two-run homer in the first inning and John Smoltz's six-hit shutout beat Pittsburgh 4-0—a cakewalk, just as Pendleton had promised. Pendleton hit .367 in the World Series; his eighth-inning double in a scoreless affair should have won Game 7 in Minnesota, but Lonnie Smith couldn't pick up the ball running from first and stopped at third.

"We still had three opportunities [to score]," said Pendleton, stranded after a 3-2-3 double play, distraught after the Twins' 1-0 triumph in the 10th. "Lonnie Smith didn't lose that for us. We wouldn't have been there if not for Lonnie Smith."

Pendleton's encore performance was also brilliant. "I thought I had a better year in '92," said Pendleton, voted an All-Star starter and Most Valuable Player runner-up after batting .311 with 21 homers, 199 hits (which tied for the most in the National League, and included an Atlanta-record 39 doubles), and a career-high 105 RBIs, second-best in the NL. In spring training, Pendleton recalls, he'd read in *Street & Smith's Baseball Yearbook*, "No way the Braves can repeat. No way Pendleton can have another career year."

"That was enough incentive for me," he said. "I told reporters in spring training, 'Who defines a career year? I don't expect to duplicate it. I expect to be better. We *did* get better. We got Deion [Sanders] on the field, with him and Otis [Nixon] out there wreaking havoc on everybody."

And Pendleton did have, to his way of thinking, an even better 1992 season than his '91 MVP campaign. "But Pittsburgh had this guy named Barry Bonds," he said, smiling. Pendleton hit just .233 in the '92 NLCS against Bonds and company. But in the decisive Game 7 in Atlanta-Fulton County Stadium, his ninth-inning double ignited a three-run rally against the Pirates. It culminated in Francisco Cabrera's two-out, two-run pinch-single for a 3-2 victory and the single most exciting moment in franchise history.

Despite a horribly slow start in 1993 (he was batting just .148 through May 4 of that season), Pendleton sizzled from then on. He hit .299 over the last 133 games, finishing at .272 for the year. Critically, he hit nine of his 17 home runs in a 25-game span from August 24 to October 1. That helped Atlanta overcome San Francisco, win a franchise-record 104 games, and capture its third straight—and final—NL West title. A third consecutive World Series, however, proved elusive. Not that it was Pendleton's fault. He sizzled in the NLCS, hitting safely in all six games against Philadelphia while batting .346 with five RBIs. Pendleton set NLCS records with 129 career at-bats and 32 games played, and set another NCLS mark with 31 straight games without an error at third base.

He started slowly again in 1994, but this time never really recovered. The worst of several early-season injuries was a bad back (after he'd already hurt his neck), prompting Pendleton to miss 37 games in that strike-shortened season. Alas, when Atlanta finally won the World Series in 1995, Pendleton wasn't there to savor what he'd helped to build toward. When the Braves didn't re-sign him due to financial considerations following the '94 season, Pendleton signed as a free agent with Florida. Atlanta, however, reacquired him in August of '96. But Pendleton got just nine at-bats in the World Series as the Braves blew a 2-0 lead and lost to the Yankees in six games.

"To win the World Series in '91 would've been icing on the cake for me. Big time," said Pendleton, who also played with Cincinnati in 1997 and Kansas City in '98, then retired and resisted the Braves' overtures for three years before returning to become their hitting coach in 2002. During this tenure, Pendleton's preferred mode of transportation to the ballpark differed from the early '90s. Just call him and Fredi Gonzalez "The Mild Bunch." Pendleton and the Braves' third-base coach often bike-pooled to work together by riding their Harley-Davidson motorcycles—just two guys on their Hogs, bandanas beneath their helmets, tooling down to Turner Field.

Indeed, it's been a long, interesting journey to Atlanta—and back again—for the man the Braves know as "TP." Never mind about that one elusive championship ring.

"I had five shots at winning a World Series," he said. "Most people don't get one.

"So, I keep preaching and teaching," said Pendleton, a devout man, a family man, and a coach who stresses patience, balance, and good hands to hitters. He still serves as a living, breathing, vivid reminder that yes, anything is possible.

GAME OF MY LIFE

"The game of my life [ended with] Sid Bream sliding home in '92—Game 7 of the NLCS. No doubt.

"I've had some great personal games myself. I remember a game against San Francisco at home, with the Braves, where I went 4-for-4 and hit two home runs. I had a double and a single, and drove in four runs and scored four. So the box score was a perfect 4, all the way across.

"In the '85 World Series with the Cardinals, I drove in two runs when we were down in Game 2, against Charlie Leibrandt. In the first game in the playoffs, there was a pop fly in foul territory that I caught, turned, and then threw home to get Jim Sundberg.

"There was the [game-tying] home run in '87 in New York that I hit off Roger McDowell [to give the Cardinals a key September win against the second-place Mets]. And, of course, Game 7 in '91 in the World Series. My goodness, that entire World Series of '91 was unbelievable.

"But Game 7 of the '92 NLCS was the game of my life. Most people won't believe me, but I felt we were going to win that game the entire game. Even when we were down 2-0 going into the bottom of the ninth. After the top of the ninth, I walked into the dugout and said, 'Boys, we've got three outs left to get it done.' I was leading off the bottom of the ninth, and I remember thinking, 'Okay, you've got to get it started.'

"I wasn't surprised when they took Doug Drabek out to start the ninth inning. No. He was exhausted. . . . That was absolutely the right move. Bringing in Stan Belinda was the right move, too. He'd been the most successful [reliever] for them all year long.

"I led off with a double. David Justice walked to the plate and hit a ground ball to the right of Jose Lind, who made an error. I thought, 'Okay, this game is ours. Let's go out and get it.' [Lind] never made an error; made three or four all year.

"Sid Bream walked in that inning to load 'em up. Ron Gant hit a sacrifice fly [to score me], and that made it 2-1. Then Damon Berryhill loaded 'em up again with another walk. Brian Hunter popped up. Then with two outs in the ninth, Francisco Cabrera hit the game-winning base hit down the left-field line. It was unbelievable.

"I told a guy next to me in the dugout, 'He's going to do it. He'll fight it off and then hit a home run. If he throws another fastball, he's gonna get it.

"On Cabera's single, I thought the ball went just to Barry Bonds' left. I thought Bonds made a perfect play. Sid would've been out if Frankie had hit the ball right at Bonds. I was standing on the top step of the dugout, and I was fired up anyway, no matter what happened. Even if Sid was thrown out, we get another inning. We were tied.

"Sid wasn't fast anymore, but Sid knew how to run the bases. A fast guy might've been out on a bang-bang play. He might have swung wide rounding third base instead of cutting it tight like Sid did. From what I could see, Sid was definitely safe. I jumped out of the dugout, and I ran over to Francisco Cabrera. Everybody was running to home plate [to Bream] and I ran to [Cabrera] at first base. He'd just rounded first, and three or four of us ran to first while everybody else dog-piled at the plate.

"Everybody can tell you where they were when that happened. It's that kind of a moment.

"I was a homebody, [so after the game] I went home. I went inside, changed, showered, and went home. My family was waiting for me. I remember sitting up all night. I helped with the kids a bit, and then they went to bed at one o'clock. Then my wife, Catherine, went to bed. But I couldn't sleep. I stayed up all night.

"I remember the next morning, the newspaper being thrown in our yard at 5:30. I was still up. I guess reading the newspaper settled me down. [I had to make] sure that it [had] happened, I guess. I finally went to bed at 7:10."

✳ ✳ ✳

Pendleton was there for the end of the Braves' historic division-title run, just as he was there for the start of it.

"We didn't win the division last year, but to have won 14 in a row is unbelievable," he said. "To sit in that dugout one day and see these [14 championship] banners hanging up out there, you say, 'Wow! That's amazing.' . . .

"The Yankees have a streak going right now. They've won, what, nine in a row? They still have to do it five more years just to equal ours. It could happen. George [Steinbrenner] could do it. But . . . they're only two-thirds of the way there.

"That's crazy."

Chapter 17

TOM GLAVINE

He was the next in succession, the rightful heir to the royal line of Aaron and Niekro and Murphy. In the heady early '90s, Tom Glavine became the face of the franchise. The babyface of the Braves, too. Irish mug, Boston bred and all, Glavine entered this world in 1966, the same year the Atlanta Braves came to town. A quarter-century hence, he became the very public face of a franchise that suddenly burst into worst-to-first prominence in 1991.

Remember? Remember how young they all looked in '91? It was especially true of Glavine, who was 25 by then yet looked, what, 21? Maybe 22? Answering to "Glav" or "Tommy," the little lefty pitched like another southpaw—"Spahnie"—that season, and for the balance of the decade. It was Glavine who gave Atlanta its only World Series title in 1995, with the considerable help of Dave Justice, who put his wallop where his mouth was. It was Glavine who, when the Braves moved into their new digs in '97, ceremoniously carried the old home plate from Atlanta-Fulton County Stadium through a hazy "Field of Dreams" outfield fog and into Turner Field. And it's Glavine who begins the 2007 season at 290 wins, and counting. With 10 more victories he will become just the 23rd pitcher in major-league history to win 300 games.

If so, Glavine will join his old teammate, close friend, and golf buddy Greg Maddux in that exclusive pitching fraternity. Once upon a time, the two alternated winning NL Cy Young Awards almost as regularly as they shared carpool driving duties to the ballpark. It seems only a matter of time and good health for Glavine to reach 300 this summer and assure his first-ballot ascension into the Baseball Hall of Fame. If that happens, he may very likely be baseball's last 300-game winner. Ever. Randy Johnson—who turns 44 this season and is coming off back surgery—and Mike Mussina—who is 38 but may not pitch beyond 40—are the only other conceivable 300 possibilities.

Glavine is the one sure thing.

* * *

Imagine if he'd kept perfecting his slapshot instead of his changeup. What if Tom Glavine had opted for hockey, not baseball? Drafted in both sports out of high school in Billerica, Massachusetts, Glavine was selected in the second round by the Braves and in the fourth round by the NHL's Los Angeles Kings. Glavine picked baseball—and hockey's loss was Atlanta's windfall.

After two full minor-league seasons, Glavine got a nine-game, late-season callup in 1987. By 1988, he was entrenched as one of Atlanta's "Young Guns," the organization's acclaimed young pitchers. The Braves were baseball's laughingstock in the late '80s; Glavine's '88 baptismal was a 7-17 shelling in which he led the National League in defeats but displayed the poise and demeanor that would come to mark his career. In 1989, Glavine went 14-8, six games over .500 on a team that finished 34 under (63-97). In an introductory look at the excellence to come, he threw four shutouts that season, tying Mark Langston for the most by a major-league left-hander. It was also the most by an Atlanta pitcher since Phil Niekro in 1978, and the most by a Braves lefty since Warren Spahn in 1963.

Pitching for another last-place team, Glavine fell to 10-12 in 1990. That season, general manager Bobby Cox took over in mid-year

for his second tenure as manager. That winter, general manager John Schuerholz came from Kansas City and orchestrated a full-scale makeover. And Tom Glavine came into his own for good as the Braves, and Atlanta, went out of this world.

"That was in many regards the most fun year," Glavine said. The year the Braves miraculously went from worst to first, from last place to top of the heap, toppled the Dodgers in the NL West, upended the Pirates for the NL pennant, then came within a whisker of winning one of the greatest World Series ever.

"Obviously, it was so unexpected," Glavine said of a season in which the Braves trailed Los Angeles by 9½ games at the All-Star break. For Dodger manager Tommy Lasorda, who was the pitchman for a dietary advertising campaign that summer, life was good. His club had taken five of seven games from Atlanta by the break. Then the second half began with a jolt. The Dodgers lost seven consecutive games and the Braves sizzled to close within 2½ games by August 10. By September, when the race was even and the Dodgers came to Atlanta, a Braves fan held up a sign; it featured a svelte Lasorda pointing to these words: "I Lost 9½ Games in Only 9 Weeks! And I Owe it All to the Braves Plan!"

On the final Saturday of the regular season, with the resurgent John Smoltz on the mound, the Braves beat Houston to clinch at least a tie for the division championship, then watched on the stadium video screen as the Dodgers lost to give Atlanta the title.

"We were just a bunch of young kids, many of whom had come up together in the organization, doing things nobody expected us to do," Glavine said. "And the city was on fire. It was such a fun year. It just ended crappy."

It ended with the Braves, after sweeping three World Series games in Atlanta to take a 3-2 lead, losing two heartbreakers back in Minneapolis to the Twins. Despite the crushing, 10-inning defeat in Game 7, that 1991 season remains the most satisfying season—and surely the most magical—to most of those '91 Braves.

"How many players would have to choose between winning a World Series and another year in picking their favorite season?" said Glavine, who calls his own decision "a tossup." For Glavine, that championship season of '95 is "the ultimate." Yet '91's near miss is a photo-finish second. "If we'd won one more game in '91," he said, "it would be the winner hands-down."

Glavine was a hands-down winner, too, that season. He easily won his first NL Cy Young Award after going 20-11, tying for the league lead in victories and complete games (nine). He was Atlanta's first 20-game winner since Niekro in '79, and had more wins by any Braves left-hander since Spahn's 23 in 1963. In becoming Atlanta's first Cy Young winner, Glavine finished second in the National League in innings pitched (246.2) and third in strikeouts (192), ERA (2.55), and opponents' batting average (.222). He was the NL's starting pitcher in his first All-Star Game and won the first of his four Silver Slugger Awards as the league's best-hitting pitcher. In four postseason decisions, Glavine lost twice to Pittsburgh and was 1-1 against the Twins, winning Game 5, 14-5, to put the Braves one win from a world championship.

"That year was kind of my coming-out party, so to speak," Glavine said, "where everything came together and I started realizing some things and figuring some things out. That was the year that certainly started my career in the direction it took."

Glavine took his game to another dimension for much of the '92 season. By mid-August, he was 19-3. In 16 starts from May 27 to August 19, Glavine compiled a 13-game winning streak, tying the franchise record set in 1884 by Charlie Buffinton.

"I pitched really well until the broken rib," said Glavine, who cracked a rib but continued to pitch in pain. "Not the smartest thing to do."

Still, he finished 20-8, tied for the NL lead with five shutouts, and started the All-Star Game for the second straight season—a first in the NL since Philadelphia Hall of Famer Robin Roberts did so in 1954-55. Glavine allowed just six home runs in the regular season. In the NL Championship Series, Glavine was beaten twice by Pittsburgh. But in the World Series opener, he beat Toronto's Jack Morris 3-1, before losing Game 4, 2-1. Glavine's two complete games made him the first left-hander to accomplish that in a World Series since Detroit's Mickey Lolich in 1968.

Lolich's Tigers, however, won that '68 Series. Glavine's Braves lost in six games in '92, and he finished second in the NL Cy Young voting to the Cubs' Maddux. He was the major league's lone 20-game winner in both '91 and '92, and the first Brave to accomplish that since Spahn in 1960-61.

"Another good year," Glavine recalled. "Another bad ending."

Another outstanding year in 1993, too. With Maddux having signed as a free agent with the Braves that winter, their rotation glittered with Glavine and Maddux, John Smoltz, and the prodigious lefty, Steve Avery—"Poison Avery," as Pittsburgh's Andy Van Slyke had called Avery during the '91 NLCS, when the kid beat the Pirates twice.

"In '93, obviously it was a great second half for us," Glavine said. Those Braves were 54-19 after the All-Star break, 54-17 once Fred McGriff arrived on July 20 after a trade with San Diego. "Every game in September was like a playoff game. We were in must-win situations so many times in September.

"Once we got in the playoffs," he said, "we were emotionally and physically drained. We were worn out going in. In many regards, that certainly was one of the best pennant races in history, and maybe the last great pennant race, before the wild card."

Glavine tied for the league lead in victories yet again, going 22-6 (a career-high .786 winning percentage) in 36 starts. He was the first National Leaguer to post three consecutive 20-victory seasons since Ferguson Jenkins compiled six from 1967-72, and beat Philadelphia in the NLCS. He finished third in the Cy Young balloting, though, behind Maddux and San Francisco's Bill Swift.

The 1994 season proved far more difficult for Glavine, and not simply due to his 13-9 mark and 3.97 ERA in 25 starts. He was the Braves' player representative, and became a prominent spokesman for the players union in the year of the short season—the players strike.

"For me personally, it was a tough time," Glavine said. "Being involved with the negotiations [with the owners] and trying to become a spokesman, to a degree. I took a lot of heat for that.

"At the time, I didn't understand it. I was trying to do my job, trying to do the best I could," he said. "I made the mistake of trying to plead our case and getting people to understand. I was a naïve kid.

"On one hand, it earned me a lot of respect," Glavine said. "On the other hand, I became a lightning rod. I took a lot of heat. [The strike] was tough for baseball. But it's made our game a better game; and we've avoided two [work-stoppage] interruptions and have [another long-term] agreement now."

Although 1994 began splendidly for the Braves, who won 13 of their first 14 games, they were six games behind the resurgent Montreal Expos in the reconfigured NL East when the strike began after 114 games. The season never resumed, however, and the Braves' streak of division titles was safe. While Glavine struggled by his standards that season, Maddux was magnificent: 16-6 with a 1.56 ERA, fully 1.12 runs lower than NL ERA-title runner-up Bret Saberhagen. The league's composite ERA was 4.21. For his efforts, Maddux was awarded his third-straight Cy Young; the following season, he would win another.

When the 1995 season finally began belatedly, Glavine immediately realized many fans had neither forgotten nor forgiven him. "I took a lot of heat, especially in Atlanta," he said. "The first game in Atlanta, I was in the bullpen. People were throwing money at me. It lasted through the summer.

"In late August, I was pitching against Cincinnati," Glavine continued. "I hit a home run in the seventh inning of a 1-1 game. We took a 2-1 lead and it was kind of the end [of much of the booing] for me. I hit a homer, I got a curtain call and thought, 'Okay, this is the end [of it] for me.'"

Although the season was shortened by 18 games that year before baseball resumed, and Glavine missed a handful of starts, he still went 16-7 in 29 starts, with a 3.08 ERA, 198 innings worked, and nine homers allowed. If Glavine was again dominant, the Braves were overwhelming. They ran away with the NL East, winning the division by 21 games. After dispatching the Colorado Rockies in four games in the inaugural NL Division Series, they swept away the Reds in the NLCS, outscoring Cincinnati 19-5 in the four-game sweep. In the World Series opener against the ascendant Indians, Maddux shut down Cleveland 3-2. His complete-game, 95-pitch gem saw just three Indians reach base—

two on opposite-field singles, the third on an error. In Game 2, it was Glavine's turn.

"I pitched okay," said Glavine, who worked six innings, giving up a two-run home run to Eddie Murray and little else in a 4-3 victory. "The big play was when Javy [Lopez, the catcher whose two-run homer in the sixth inning proved decisive] picked off Manny Ramirez at first. It ended the [sixth] inning when I was in trouble. Then we took control.

"Earlier in my career, I would have lost that game," he said. "After 1991, those were the kind of games I learned how to win. And they make you a 20-game winner, or a 15-game winner, instead of a .500 pitcher."

Game 6 made Glavine a pitcher Braves fans will never forget.

GAME OF MY LIFE

"Game 6 of the 1995 World Series, that's my defining game. That's the greatest game I pitched. I guess from a pitching standpoint, statistically, it's as good or maybe better than any game I've ever had. But when you combine the whole package—what the game meant . . . and what we'd all gone through—that's as good as it gets. To pitch that game, in that situation, that's the greatest thing I could have asked for.

"I guess for me, there were a lot of emotions going through my head in that game. We had had a chance to win the World Series in Game 5. As a player, when you have an opportunity to win it all, you want to win it and put it to bed. I wanted it, I wanted that opportunity. But when you're a pitcher and you're looking at a situation like Game 5, you go through the disappointment of not winning the series. You have to start gearing up to pitch a game you hoped you wouldn't have to pitch.

"It really kind of hit me when we flew back from Cleveland to Atlanta and we landed. And I realized I had to pitch. I looked at it as a great opportunity, though, not a disappointment. It was the game that helped provide the championship we all wanted desperately.

"I started to embrace the opportunity. I knew I had good stuff warming up in the bullpen. But for me, so many times, well, you just don't know. But I warmed up well that night. Everything was crisp. You try to carry everything over [from the bullpen to the mound]. The first inning for me has always been my Achilles heel. But when I got through the first inning that night, I thought, 'Okay, that's the same stuff I had in the bullpen. Here we go.'

"I never envisioned throwing a one-hitter, of course. That's the most dangerous, most balanced lineup I ever faced. Even their seventh-place hitter, Jim Thome, had 30 home runs.

"As each inning went on, and I got through it and I hadn't given up a hit yet, everything was snowballing. I got more and more confident. I was in the zone. Then David [Justice] gave us the big hit.

"In the top of the sixth inning, Tony Pena blooped a changeup over Lemmer's [second baseman Mark Lemke] head. It was the first time I'd faced any kind of adversity that night, but I got through that inning.

"The no-hitter was certainly out there, but I didn't anticipate it. In that setting, [losing the no-hitter was] probably a release. I didn't have to worry about it. I was kind of feeling good about myself. I came into the dugout after Pena's hit and I remember screaming, 'Just get me one! 'Cause they're not getting any runs tonight!' As a pitcher, you sometimes say things to rally the troops. It just so happened it worked that time. David hit the home run.

"In the ninth inning, Mark [Wohlers, the closer] is in, and I just remember sitting there in the dugout, knowing we were on the verge of doing what we wanted to do—finally winning the World Series. It's just an eternity for that inning to end. It's taking forever: 'Come on, hurry up!' I thought to myself.

"I think the key to that inning was Raffy [Belliard] running down the line to get [leadoff man Kenny] Lofton's ball. The key was to keep Lofton off base. We get the next out, and then there's that fly ball to center.

"In the short time it took for that ball to settle into [center fielder] Marquis [Grissom's] glove, there were so many emotions. I played it out from the start of the season. This is what we came to spring training for, to win the World Series and to run out on the field with my buddies.

"We'd had so many disappointments. We had this group of guys, all these guys who'd played together and been around each other in the system and then the major leagues, and we'd finally tasted success after so many disappointments. That's what made it so special."

✳ ✳ ✳

Glavine was named the Most Valuable Player of the 1995 World Series. Don Larsen's legacy as the only man to pitch a perfect game in the World Series was secure, but Glavine was magnificent against Cleveland—2-0 with a 1.29 ERA in 14 innings pitched. Of his 11 strikeouts, eight came in the decisive Game 6.

In '96, Glavine won 15 games, with a 2.98 ERA. In the postseason, he won the clincher in both the NL Division Series and the NLCS: A 5-2 win over Los Angeles in Game 3, including a two-out double in a decisive four-run fourth inning; and a two-out, three-run triple in Game 7 of the NLCS as Atlanta won 15-0 for its third straight victory over St. Louis after trailing 3-1 in games. The World Series would be another matter, however. It remains so to this day.

"That was the one to me," Glavine said. "People always ask, 'Which World Series was the one you should've won?' That was the one Series that we blew.

"To go into New York and win two games up there," he said. "Then come home, lose three, then lose again in New York. Two of the games we had won. That's the one I really think we blew, the one we should've won."

Especially when Atlanta took a 6-0 lead in Game 4, only to see Denny Neagle surrender half of that lead to the Yankees. Then Jim Leyritz teed off on Wohlers' slider in the eighth inning for a tying, three-run pinch homer. New York won it 8-6 in 10 innings, and Atlanta never recovered, losing 1-0 in Game 5, then 3-2 in Game 6 in Yankee Stadium.

"Had we won that series, you'd hear none of that talk about the Braves winning only one World Series," Glavine said. "The team and the organization would've had the respect we deserved.

"You won't find a player who wouldn't want to play on a team that won the division every year, even if they only won one World Series," he said. "The 11 division titles when I was there, the 14 [consecutive] total, that's not something you're going to see again. The only team with a remote chance of matching that is the Yankees, and they've got, what, five more to go?

"Any time a team does something that's never been done in any sport, that's pretty special. But there's no question the team doesn't get the credit for what it's done."

No question, either, that Glavine knows this, too: "Would you rather be the Florida Marlins, or even the Toronto Blue Jays, who won two World Series, but everything in between was terrible? Or would you rather win 14 straight championships and only win the Series once? Almost every player I've ever talked to said he'd rather be on a team that won the division every year."

After winning 14 games in 1997, Glavine won his second Cy Young Award in '98 by going 20-6, his fourth 20-win season, with a career-low 2.47 earned run average. Glavine was just 14-11 in '99, but the Braves returned to the World Series (only to be swept in four games by the Yankees). He led the majors with 21 victories in 2000, but finished second to Arizona's Randy Johnson for the Cy Young.

A 16-7 season in 2001 was punctuated by eight scoreless innings of work in an NLDS win over Houston. Glavine gave Atlanta its only victory over Arizona in the NLCS, but was the loser in the decisive Game 5. He would lose twice to the Giants, however, in the 2002 NLDS. But it would be four more Octobers before the second-winningest pitcher in postseason history would win another playoff game.

"Leaving Atlanta was the hardest thing I've ever done," said Glavine, a free agent after the 2002 season who was so angered by Atlanta's negotiating ploys that he signed a four-year deal with the New York Mets. "Not so much for me, but what it did to my family."

To his wife, Christine, and four children: their two young sons, Peyton and Mason, Glavine's daughter Amber by his first wife, Chris' son Jonathan from her first marriage. The move to the Mets was a wrenching one for the Glavine family. The 2003 Mets themselves were abysmal, which also contributed mightily to Glavine's 9-14 record that season. After starting off the year 5-2 in New York, Glavine was blistered by the Braves upon his return to Turner Field. His former teammates were so familiar with him: how he pounded the outside corner, low and away, a call he'd always gotten from umpires, but not now with the new QuesTec cameras and Major League Baseball forcing the umpires to adapt their strike zone. The abrupt change confounded Glavine, whose control went awry and whose circle-change was far less effective when he found himself pitching behind in the count so often.

In Atlanta, the crowds were vicious toward Glavine and his family, who still live in the northern suburb of Alpharetta. Many remembered the strike. Many were angry that Glavine had signed with the Mets. He was booed and jeered and cursed—starting on May 24, 2003, when Glavine was rocked for six runs and eight hits (including two homers) in just 3⅓ innings of that 10-4 loss. Peyton cried that day while watching his father pitch. Chris never brought the kids back to Turner Field again that season.

The Braves continued to beat up on their former face and leader. Glavine's second season wasn't much better, 11-14, though his ERA dropped from 4.52 to 3.60. After three seasons in Flushing, he was just 2-8 against Atlanta. But after opening the 2005 season 1-4, Glavine—at the urging of Mets pitching coach Rick Peterson—changed his approach. He became more aggressive, pitching inside, jamming right-handed hitters, relying less exclusively on his circle-change and more on his fastball. He pounded the strike zone and finished the season 13-13. That season, he allowed just 12 homers (his lowest total since 1995). At age 39, in his last three starts of '05, he worked 26 innings. The last time he'd pitched 26 innings over a three-start span: June 29-July 14, 1991, his first Cy Young season. The first nine of those 26 innings? A complete-game, 4-1 victory over Atlanta.

"My family enjoyed the time in New York, made the most of it," said Glavine, who bought a house in Greenwich, Connecticut, where his parents, Fred and Millie, often lived during the season and where Chris and the kids stayed during the summer. "But the first two years were hard.

"I went from being on a championship team to being on a team that was out of contention by Memorial Day weekend," he said. "That was hard. But this past year was a great year. It's the reason why I went to New York. It was awesome."

After starting the 2006 season 2-2 (including a 2-1 loss to the Braves), Glavine kick-started his full-fledged comeback campaign on April 29 with seven shutout innings in a 1-0 victory in Atlanta. It was the first of nine consecutive triumphs for Glavine—his longest winning streak since the 13-gamer in '92. He was an early Cy Young front-runner, an All-Star for the 10th time. Glavine finished the season 15-7, with an ERA of 3.82. He survived a late-season scare: coldness in his left ring finger, and a blood clot scare in his left shoulder that might have required season-ending—and possibly career-threatening—surgery. Instead, Glavine took aspirin, returned to form, and in time to oust the Dodgers in Game 2 of the NLDS. "Tom Terrific," the back page of *Newsday* heralded him, harking back to the days of the original Tom Terrific, Hall of Famer and 300-game winner Tom Seaver of the '69 Miracle Mets.

Glavine then beat St. Louis 2-0 in Game 1 of the NL Championship Series. "Big Game Tommy," his manager, Willie Randolph, called Glavine, whose 14th postseason victory enabled him to tie Andy Pettitte for second-most wins in the postseason behind John Smoltz (15). Glavine is still stuck at 14 after losing to the Cardinals in Game 5 of the NLCS. The Mets ended up losing the series to the Cardinals after Yadier Molina's dramatic home run rallied St. Louis in Game 7.

"In the end, it was like some of the [postseason] games we had in Atlanta," Glavine said. "One different play, a big hit, and we would've been in the World Series."

By Thanksgiving, he was already anticipating a return to yet another World Series. With his 41st birthday coming on March 25, with him pitching as well as he has in years, Glavine became a free agent once again. He was debating whether to re-sign with the Mets, or return home to the Braves. And with his 300th victory clearly on the horizon, only one question remained: Whose uniform would Tom Glavine be wearing when that moment finally comes?

Unfortunately for Atlanta, Glavine chose to resign with the Mets, John Schuerholz and the Braves didn't tender an offer by the deadline Glavine had imposed in fairness to New York. So his 300th victory will come in a Mets uniform, Braves fans can take solace in this: 242 of Glavine's career victories came with an A on his cap.

Chapter 18

CHARLIE LEIBRANDT

He was the self-proclaimed "old guy" in the Braves' 1991 and '92 rotations. The geezer—make that wizened veteran—among the "Young Guns" who began Atlanta's run of excellence. Charlie Leibrandt was a 15-game winner for each of those two National League pennant winners. Yet unfortunately, he's remembered by many for two rare relief appearances, and the part he played in Atlanta losing the '91 and '92 World Series.

"A couple of my good friends, golfing buddies, still give me a hard time about it," Leibrandt said. "You've got to be remembered for something, I guess."

For two things, actually: the 11th-inning, game-winning home run Leibrandt gave up to Minnesota's Kirby Puckett in Game 6 of the '91 World Series; and the following season, in Game 6 of the 1992 World Series, the two-out, two-run double he surrendered to Dave Winfield in the 11th.

Both times Leibrandt was the loser, but he's not a sore one. "I've got a lot more to be proud of than ashamed of," said Leibrandt.

Indeed. The left-hander was 140-119 in 14 major-league seasons, including a 39-31 record in his three seasons with Atlanta. After starting his career with Cincinnati, Leibrandt pitched six seasons in Kansas City. In 1985, he was 17-9, with a 2.69 earned-run average as the Royals won the World Series. Leibrandt finished fifth in the AL Cy Young voting that year.

After going 5-11 in 1989, however, Leibrandt was traded to Atlanta. "I needed a change of scenery," he said, "so it was good to go somewhere I was wanted. I'd had some good years in Kansas City, but it was time to turn the page. Atlanta wanted me, so it was a new challenge."

It would prove to be a severe challenge, at least initially. In the previous five seasons, Atlanta had won more than 70 games just once. "When I was traded, I wasn't too excited to come here," said Leibrandt, who still lives in the Atlanta area, dabbles in real estate, and is the volunteer pitching coach at The Marist School, which two of his four children attend. "I didn't know much about Atlanta or the South, and the team didn't seem to be too good.

"And we weren't very good," Leibrandt said of those 1990 Braves, who finished 65-97. "But you could see some potential from a lot of young guys.

"I was probably 10 years older [than the rest of Atlanta's young starting pitchers]," said Leibrandt, the No. 4 starter in the '91 and '92 rotations. "I was definitely the old guy on a couple of teams. We had Smoltz, Glavine, and Avery. It was still surprising, because none of the guys except for Smoltz were the Nolan Ryan types. You always think the guys will be good, but you never know.

"Those guys were confident," he said. "They knew what they wanted to do and did it."

That was due, in part, to Leibrandt, a craftsman who helped John Smoltz, Tom Glavine, and Steve Avery develop, and who showed them that pitchers can outsmart hitters without having to overpower them. "As a veteran pitcher," he said, "I always felt it was my responsibility to mentor guys, whether to talk to them or show them on the mound."

Yet no one could foresee Atlanta's dramatic turnaround in 1991, in Bobby Cox's second tenure as manager of the Braves. "Oh, no. I don't think anybody could," Leibrandt said. "That's why it's so special. The town was starved for a winner.

"But as the season kept moving along," he said, "and we kept being more competitive and the Dodgers kept struggling, we got hot and the town got behind us and we really started believing in ourselves."

In September, and on into October, Atlanta fans were fanatic. Deliriously, joyously so. "The Tomahawk Chop" was everywhere. "Kansas City was behind [us when I pitched there]; we had good baseball fans there, but I'd never seen anything like it [in Atlanta]," Leibrandt said. "All anybody wanted to do was talk about the Atlanta Braves.

"People stayed up until one or two in the morning to watch us on the West Coast," he said. "It seemed like anywhere I went—to the supermarket, to buy gas—people recognized me and said, 'Hey, keep it up, we're watching you.'"

After clinching the NL Western Division, the Braves won Games 6 and 7 of the NLCS in Pittsburgh. On a raucous flight to Minnesota, Leibrandt learned he would start Game 1 of the World Series two nights later. He lost it, getting knocked out in the fifth inning of that 5-2 defeat. But it's Game 6 for which Charlie Leibrandt's best remembered. The Braves were a victory away from their first world championship since 1957. With the score 3-3, Cox brought in Leibrandt for his first relief appearance as a Brave, Atlanta's third reliever of the night after Mike Stanton and closer Alejandro Pena had each worked two scoreless innings.

"I wasn't surprised. Whether I should have been out there, I don't know," Leibrandt said. "But we didn't have a lot of experience in our bullpen. We were pretty green. As the game went on, I looked down the bench and thought, 'I'm the guy who's probably going in next.'"

Puckett, leading off, lined a home run on Leibrandt's second pitch to force a Game 7. It cleared the left-field wall, where in the third inning Puckett had made a leaping catch above the wall with a runner on base.

"Why not Leibrandt?" Cox said after that crushing 4-3 loss. "We'd be pretty stupid if we were resistant to bringing in a 15-game winner."

"It certainly wasn't the highlight of my career," Leibrandt said. "I was happy to be out there and get the ball. I wanted to compete, and didn't."

That regular season, Leibrandt, Glavine, and Avery each won at least 15 games, the first time three left-handers on a team had done so since the 1917 New York Giants. Leibrandt won 15 again in '92, but the lasting memory is the last batter he faced as a Brave. Again in relief, after retiring the Blue Jays in the 10th inning in Game 6 of the World Series, "I got in trouble in the 11th," Leibrandt said. "I didn't make a very good pitch to Winfield, and he got a double."

"I was happy to get in and hoping to do a better job," said Leibrandt, who was traded to Texas that winter once the Braves signed free agent Greg Maddux, and then pitched his last season for the Rangers. "If we'd scored in the bottom of the 10th, I could've been a hero. But I am who I am. That's okay. To pitch as long as I did, that's great."

Leibrandt, who turned 50 in October, is now imparting much of what he learned in a 14-year big-league career to a promising young player—his son, Brodie, a junior at Marist. "Believe it or not, he's a left-handed pitcher," Leibrandt said, chuckling about his offspring, who favors his famous father in more ways than one.

"Yeah, he's crafty," Leibrandt said, smiling. "That's what they say about left-handers. You don't overpower people. That's why I enjoy watching Tom Glavine pitch. I played with Kenny Rogers, too, in Texas."

That's why Leibrandt appreciated watching Glavine and Rogers pitch so well—Glavine for the New York Mets, Rogers for the resurgent Detroit Tigers—in the 2006 playoffs.

"What these guys are doing at that age, pitching as well—or better—than they ever have, is unbelievable," Leibrandt said of the two 40-somethings. "It's a testament to how hard they work. And both of these guys are really tough. Both want to win. And they both keep themselves in shape.

"I think Glav is a more complete pitcher now," said Leibrandt, who stays in shape himself partly by playing golf regularly. "Tom pitches to both sides of the plate now, not just away but inside, too. When you get older, you have to adjust."

GAME OF MY LIFE

"Probably my best game was in the mid-'80s when I threw a one-hit shutout against the Milwaukee Brewers. The only hit was a bunt single in about the sixth inning. There was a little controversy at the time, too.

"The game wasn't close, probably 6- or 8-0. The Brewers had a big catcher; his last name was Schroeder [Bill Schroeder, a lifetime .240 hitter]. He bunted on me. Nobody was expecting it, and it was the only hit of the game. That was my best game.

"Now, as far as my most memorable game, well, I pitched a lot of good playoff games with Kansas City. In one game, I was coming in in relief in 1985 against, ironically, Bobby Cox. Bobby was managing Toronto and this was in the ALCS."

[In that series, the first year Major League Baseball had expanded the LCS from five games to a best-of-seven series, Leibrandt was the starter, and loser, in Games 1 and 4. In Game 4 in Kansas City, Leibrandt gave way to closer Dan Quisenberry in the ninth inning, when the Blue Jays scored three runs to win 3-1 and take a 3-1 lead in the series. Kansas City won the next two games to even the ALCS; then came the decisive Game 7 in Toronto.]

"Bret Saberhagen started for us, and he got hit in the hand in the first or second inning. Bret was a good athlete; he probably used his bare hand to field the ball. An inning or so later, his right hand was all puffed up.

"It was one of those nice days in Toronto, probably 38 degrees. I came on in relief [in the fourth inning] and pitched through the eighth, five innings of shutout ball."

[Actually, Leibrandt allowed one run in the sixth inning, when the Blue Jays cut the lead to 2-1. But after Jim Sundberg's wind-blown triple in KC's four-run sixth inning, the Royals carried a 6-1 lead into the ninth inning.]

"I started the ninth and gave up a hit or two, and then Dan Quisenberry came in. Quiz shut them down, and that was the year we went on to win the World Series—our first and only World Series [championship].

"I started Game 2 against St. Louis, and had a low-hit game going, leading going into the ninth inning. [Leibrandt worked eight shutout innings, allowing the Cardinals but two hits, and took a 2-0 lead into the ninth inning]. I end up getting two outs in the ninth, no runners on. But the Cardinals loaded the bases, and then Terry Pendleton gets a bloop double down the line. That clears the bases, and we lose 4-2.

"I pitched Game 6 and St. Louis scored a run off me in the top of the eighth to take a 1-0 lead. Then we scored twice in the ninth inning. Yes, that was the Denkinger game."

[In that game, first base umpire Don Denkinger blew a call that likely deprived St. Louis of a world championship. With Todd Worrell pitching in relief of Cards' starter Danny Cox, Royals' pinch hitter Jorge Orta was ruled safe at first base on a grounder that, TV replay cameras clearly showed, should have been called an out. Denkinger simply missed the call, and St. Louis manager Whitey Herzog vehemently argued to no avail. After a single and a passed ball, an intentional walk loaded the bases and set up a double play. But Dane Iorg's two-run, pinch-hit single off Worrell won it, 2-1, to force a decisive seventh game and insure Denkinger's blown call would live in baseball infamy.]

"Then we won Game 7 and the World Series."

✳ ✳ ✳

When the Braves' record streak of 14 consecutive division titles finally ended last fall, Leibrandt was a dozen years removed from his Atlanta playing days. That certainly didn't diminish his pride in, and appreciation of, the Braves' record run.

"It's a phenomenal achievement," said Leibrandt. "To do it 14 years in a row, with a lot of different personnel, that's not easy. It's a testament to Bobby Cox and his staff, and to John Schuerholz.

"It's disappointing we didn't win another [World Series]," he said. "We were favored in a lot of them early. In the last several years, Atlanta hasn't been as strong as the Braves once were. We could've won several, but in the last few years the Braves haven't been as good. Look at the Yankees; they're the best team money can buy, and they haven't won it all since 2000."

Winning a World Series, Leibrandt knows, is anything but easy. "You've got to be at your best, and hot," he said. "You've got to get great pitching, and you've got to get key hits. The biggest problem here in Atlanta is we didn't get enough key hits at crucial times.

"We had our chance in Minnesota in '91," Leibrandt said. "We had a chance against Toronto in '92. But I guess they were better. If we'd won just one more [world championship], it would've changed everybody's mind about the Braves."

Chapter 19

JEFF BLAUSER

One of the most memorable photos of the Atlanta Braves' rise to prominence was taken by team photographer Walter Victor on July 18, 1993, the night Fred McGriff arrived in a trade that changed the face—and significantly raised the temperature—of an already scintillating pennant race. It was also the night the press box in Atlanta-Fulton County Stadium caught fire during batting practice, providing an intriguing backdrop for the memorable photograph.

Down on the field, as the flames roared and black smoke billowed out of the press box during BP, the two buddies posed with their arms around each other's shoulders: Jeff Blauser and Mark Lemke, the middle infield combo for much of the '90s. Victor clicked, and his photo eventually found its way to Cooperstown and the Baseball Hall of Fame.

If Lemke was, as manager Bobby Cox called him, "The original dirt player," then Blauser was "The Bud Man." It was his chin, a Mt. Rushmore of a chin, one as prominent as that of the Budweiser cartoon character featured in a series of advertisements and TV commercials. Of the four opening-day shortstops during Atlanta's 14-year run of division titles, The Bud Man was the most dependable—and durable, too.

The Bud Man always kept his chin up. The irony, of course, is that Blauser was unable to play when Atlanta finally won the World Series in 1995. It is one of his few baseball regrets. In the 1995 NLCS, in which Atlanta swept Cincinnati in four games, Blauser was injured while trying to turn a doubleplay.

"Hal Morris hit me in the thigh," he recalled. "He slid in and caught me with an elbow. You know how football players get thigh bruises? I had a bad hematoma. More than once we had to go in with a long needle to draw the blood out so it wouldn't calcify."

Blauser only played in Game 1 of the NLCS, giving way to Rafael Belliard. When it came time to set Atlanta's World Series roster, Blauser wasn't on it. He knew he couldn't, and shouldn't, play. "But I didn't feel like I wasn't part of it," Blauser said. "I was. Everybody feels that. That's just the way it goes. I could've been very selfish and said, 'Yeah, I can play.' But that wouldn't have been fair to my teammates and to the organization, if I played when I wasn't even 50 percent. I knew I wasn't as [healthy] as someone else.

"You have to have the courage to swallow your pride and say, 'Hey, someone else is better than me now,'" Blauser said. "That's life. That's how it goes."

So during the World Series, Blauser watched as Belliard played short, and the Braves beat the Cleveland Indians in six games for Atlanta's first—and only—world championship.

"We should've had more—or we were in a position to win more," Blauser said. "This is America. If you win two, everyone thinks you should have won three. There's always going to be people who probably say we weren't successful enough—the half-empty, half-full thing. But I don't think anybody who played on those teams looks at what we didn't accomplish, but what we did."

The Bud Man was an organization man. The club's first pick in the 1984 secondary draft, Blauser advanced through the system, had call-ups in 1987 and '88, before reaching the majors for good in '89. A shortstop, Blauser also played second and third base, even some

outfield, before returning to shortstop for good in 1991. But Belliard, the sweet-fielding, weak-hitting shortstop acquired in a trade with Pittsburgh, was the starter for most of that magical season.

"Raffy was a better defensive player than I was at that time," Blauser said. "It was like I was the 10th starter. I didn't know when I'd get in there, but a lot of times it was early."

For Blauser, the miraculous 1991 season will always be "the most special," he said. "More than anything, I remember the electricity every day at the stadium. It's kind of a cliché, but you really could feel it. And the aura about that team, that stadium, the fans, it made the hair stand up on the back of your neck."

Blauser was on the field in the 11th inning of Game 6 of the World Series, when Kirby Puckett homered off Charlie Liebrandt to force a Game 7 in the Metrodome. "I remember that sinking feeling," he said. "I remember how hard it was, and to walk off that field it seemed like a mile."

He was there again for Game 7, when the Twins won the world championship 1-0 in the bottom of the 10th inning. "I remember how crushed everybody was," said Blauser. "But there was tremendous pride in the accomplishment, how far we'd come."

During the 1992 season, Blauser eventually supplanted Belliard as the regular shortstop. That July 12, in Wrigley Field, Blauser became the fourth shortstop in the modern era to hit three homers in a game. That August, he hit the Braves' first inside-the-park homer in nearly 20 years. In October of '92, Blauser appeared in another famous photo: in an Atlanta mosh pit, the human pileup at home plate after Sid Bream scored the winning run on Francisco Cabrera's pinch-hit single in the bottom of the ninth to stun Pittsburgh in Game 7 of the NLCS.

"Everybody talks about that," said Blauser, who has a framed photo of that delirious celebration in his home. "That's the subject that's probably brought up most often—Sid Bream."

In 1993, Blauser took over at shortstop for good and had a break-out season. He batted .305, the first Braves shortstop to hit over .300 since Alvin Dark in 1948. Blauser blossomed defensively, too, and was named to the NL All-Star team for the first time (he was also an All-

Star in 1997). He played 161 games, scored 110 runs, and set an Atlanta record for fielding percentage by a shortstop (.970). But the Braves, exhausted by their dramatic, prolonged chase of San Francisco in the NL West race, lost the NL Championship Series to Philadelphia in six games.

After the players' strike curtailed the 1994 season, Blauser could only watch as Atlanta won the 1995 series. When the Braves swept the first two games in the '96 series in Yankee Stadium, a second straight world championship seemed almost inevitable.

"Have we ever gone into the World Series up until '96 as the consensus favorite? Probably not," Blauser said. "When we went up 2-0, Mark Bradley wrote in the *Journal-Constitution*, 'It's over.' We had a workout that day. You could sense in the clubhouse that we didn't want to have that written. We didn't feel that way. We saw that headline and said, 'Oh, no. That's bad.'"

Prophetic, too. The Yankees swept all three games in Atlanta. David Cone beat Tom Glavine, 5-2, in Game 3 before Mark Wohlers threw that fateful, series-changing slider to Jim Leyritz in Game 4. After Andy Pettitte outdueled John Smoltz, 1-0, in Game 5, the Yankees flew home to the Bronx, scored three runs off Greg Maddux in the third inning of Game 6, and went on to win 3-2 for their first World Series title since 1981.

In 1997, the Braves first year in their new Turner Field home, Blauser had another superb, timely season. In the last year of his contract, he hit a career-high .308 with 17 homers and 70 RBIs. "I was healthy again," Blauser said. "Everything fell into place. I felt like I had a horseshoe with me.

"Everything turned to gold for me," he said. "It was a tremendous satisfaction, after all the negative press I had in '95 and '96 [when he'd hit .211 and .245, respectively]."

Unfortunately, with Blauser a free agent, his agent, Scott Boras, "Threw out some numbers," Blauser recalled. "I didn't want to go anywhere." Blauser ended up signing a two-year contract with the Cubs for essentially the same money Boras tossed at the Braves.

"It meant more to me to stay here and be with a winner," said Blauser, who still lives in the Atlanta suburb of Alpharetta, with his wife, Andee, and their children, Abbie, six, and Cooper, three. "For a time, I was sad about it. But with the Cubs, I saw all that Sammy Sosa-Mark McGwire [home run] stuff. The Cubs, at the time, were kind of like we were in '91; they didn't know they were supposed to win."

The Cubs won the wild card, only to lose to Atlanta in the NL Division Series. After the '99 season, Blauser retired. In his 13-year major-league career, he batted .262 with 122 home runs and 513 RBIs. He was hit by pitches 91 times in his career, and grounded into double plays only 77 times. Blauser's career fielding average stands at .962, with just 188 errors in nearly 5,000 chances.

Starting in 2003, Blauser was a roving minor-league infield instructor in the Braves' farm system. "I enjoyed being with the minor-league guys," he said, "trying to teach guys what we learned at the major-league level and to play for the name on the front of the shirt, not for the name on the back—not for themselves. To be a winner. That's fun.

"When I played, I played hurt, knowing I was going to suffer personally," Blauser said. "But it was important for me to get out there for the team. I see a lot of players in the minor leagues now who get a little banged up and don't play. I try to show them. I do have a debt to the organization. I owe them my knowledge to the young kids."

In the 2006 season, Blauser imparted even more knowledge as manager of the Mississippi Braves, Atlanta's Class AA affiliate in the Southern League that is based in Jackson, Mississippi. "When Dayton Moore was still here [as Atlanta's assistant general manager for baseball operations, before being named the Kansas City Royals' general manager midway through last season], he'd actually asked me several years in a row to manage," Blauser said. When Moore approached Blauser one day late in the 2005 season, the Bud Man finally acquiesced.

"With my little girl in school, I thought it'd be better [timing for the family]," Blauser said. "It was a tremendous opportunity. So I thought I'd try it for a year and see how it worked out."

His wife, Andee, is from Louisiana, and has several relatives there, including a sister in New Orleans. But Andee and the children continued to live in Alpharetta most of the season, making the five- to six-hour drive to Jackson.

"For me, it was a big learning experience," said Blauser. "Not only learning about myself, but the young players. There's a different mind-set among young players today, certainly different than what I expected.

"What changes today is the attention some young players get," he said. "There's a lot of attention, from [publications like] *Baseball America*. Most of these guys have agents, too. They're signed, and some are on the 40-man roster. It changes things. It's different. It takes away from the close-knit, us-against-the-world feeling we had in the minors. They have to be businessmen. Some even have shoe [endorsement] contracts."

It's much different than when Blauser was making his way up the Braves' organizational ladder to Atlanta. "It's a lot different atmosphere now," he said. "You were in this small town, had no luxuries. We relied on each other." Blauser says that many players have distorted expectations for the minor leagues; they expect to make one stop on the franchise food chain each season, climbing a rung annually until reaching the majors. "The cold truth is, it's not always that way," said Blauser, who managed a few players—"repeat guys" he calls them—who were playing in Jackson for a second consecutive season. "I recall some guys I played with in the minor leagues, they hit 20 homers, hit .280, and never got out of A ball."

Unlike his days in Double-A, the 21st-century amenities—even in the lower minors—are much improved. "These guys have it made," Blauser said. "They've got great facilities. They've got great spreads [of food in the clubhouse].

"I learned a lot about myself, too," he said. "How to push the right buttons on different guys. Each individual, they all respond to different things. I had several guys, it was their first year state-side. They were adjusting not only to baseball, but to life in a Southern town."

In the first half of the Southern League season, Blauser's Braves finished third in the league's five-team South Division. In the second half, they finished last at 27-42, 13-1/2 games out of first.

"In the minors, it's about getting the players to [advance to] the next level," he said. "I understand that. At the same time, it's a daily juggling act, preparing these guys for the next level but also going out and trying to win. Some guys learn one important thing for the season. For others, there's a handful of things they learn, one at a time, then another.

"The most exciting thing at the end of the day, "Blauser said, "is to see a player [do something] in a game we've been working on."

Blauser will continue doing that in 2007, just not on a regular basis in Mississippi. He won't be managing the Double-A Braves again, a decision that's far more personal than professional. "I will not likely be moving again," Blauser said. "With the family, it takes a pretty heavy toll. I'd rather raise my children and be proactive with that, than raising somebody else's children.

"It's still a juggling act," he said. "I've had my day in the sun, getting attention [as a player]. So I can put that on the back burner. That's our legacy—[our] children—when we're dead and gone. Don't get me wrong. I still love the game. I'd still get butterflies at seven o'clock each night before the first pitch."

For now, however, for the foreseeable future, Blauser sees himself at Abbie's after-school activities and Cooper's tee-ball games.

"I told Paul Snyder [re-hired in September as Atlanta's director of baseball operations] that I'm not considering myself done with managing," Blauser said. "I can see getting back into it in a couple of years."

GAME OF MY LIFE

"I'd have to say that the game [on July 12, 1992] I hit three home runs in was, on a lot of different levels, a special day.

"First, it was a right-handed starting pitcher that day, the day before the All-Star [break]. Up until that time, I hadn't started against right-handed pitchers. Raffy [Belliard] would start against right-handers, and I'd start against left-handers. Frank Castillo was starting that day for the Cubs. I hit three homers, and I hit the third one against Paul Assenmacher, who was a Brave and is now one of my neighbors.

"When I see people now and they recognize me and they want to talk baseball, nine out of 10 times they bring up the three-homer game. In 1992, there wasn't much cable TV [games] then. WGN was really it; if you were going to watch baseball that day, you watched the Cubs.

"Just being there, too, was important. That's the culmination of everything I wanted to do. I wasn't one of those kids who wanted to grow up and be president, or an astronaut, or a firefighter. I wanted to be a baseball player. I had a one-track mind.

"Why did I start against a right-hander that day? I think Ned Yost [a Braves coach and close friend of Blauser's, and now the manager of the Milwaukee Brewers], since it was the day before the All-Star Game, said to Bobby Cox, 'Let Blaus play.' Ned would do that to Bobby, and sometimes Bobby does that, lets other guys play.

"My thinking was, 'You're not gonna start today. Oh, they've got two left-handers going in this series, so I'll start one out of three games.' A lot of times that year, though, I'd be in the game by the third inning. Even if I didn't start, I'd be in. A lot of times, Raffy would start and play two innings, and I'd pinch hit for him.

"I always enjoyed playing at Wrigley Field, too. There's no finer place to play than Wrigley—in the day, during the summer. My third homer was the game-winner, in the 10th inning. I remember telling Clarence Jones, our hitting coach, 'Aussie's going to throw a little roundhouse curve.' He always did, for a strike. It was a cross between an eephus pitch and a good curveball. I said, 'C.J., I'm going to hit a home run.' And I did."

Chapter 20

DALE MURPHY

I f Stan Musial was, as the plaque on the statue of Stan the Man outside Busch Stadium attests, "Baseball's perfect knight," then Dale Murphy was baseball's Boy Scout ideal. He didn't drink alcohol and he's never smoked a cigarette. Profanity? Please.

On the field, he was nearly as perfect. When the Gold Glove, slugging center fielder earned the game's most distinguished merit badge—the National League Most Valuable Player Award—in the 1982 and '83 seasons, he became the youngest player ever to do so.

Once, in an ideal confluence of man and marketing, the devout Mormon everyone called "Murph" even made his pitch for . . . milk. Got Murph? Atlanta did. And for the longest time later in the interminable, infernal '80s, Murph was the Braves' only blessed attribute. As then-club president Stan Kasten said in the summer of 2000, during Murphy's induction into the Braves Hall of Fame, "That's a heavy burden to hang on anyone, to be the symbol of the Atlanta Braves during [the 1980s]. For that decade, you were all we had."

Even Murphy's presence that steamy August day was, well, vintage Murph. He was gracious, self-deprecating, and, at times, emotional. Murphy was supposed to be inducted into the Braves hall with the previous year's inaugural class. As a player, he was in a class with those men: Hank Aaron, Eddie Mathews, Phil Niekro, and Warren Spahn, all also enshrined in Cooperstown. But Murphy asked for a year's delay, in order to complete a three-year Mormon mission in Boston.

Got Murph? Cooperstown doesn't, likely never will, and is the worse for it. Murphy's been on the Hall of Fame ballot since 1998, but hasn't really come close to being elected. The main culprit? A .265 career batting average. Yet he walloped 398 home runs, and won five consecutive Gold Gloves as a converted catcher-turned-first baseman-turned center fielder. Murphy was 26, then 27 when he won his successive MVPs. He was a seven-time NL All-Star, each time a starter, including six straight seasons from 1982-87. He was a 30-30 player when hitting 30 homers and stealing 30 bases really meant something. He once played in 740 consecutive games, and was honored with baseball's Lou Gehrig Memorial Award and the Roberto Clemente Award for his good works.

Above and beyond all that, there's the man himself. As Thomas Stinson of the *Atlanta Journal-Constitution* wrote in 2000, after visiting Murphy at his home in Alpine, Utah: "The most enduring qualities remain untouched—the absence of ego, the disarming presence, the ability to make people around him feel good without saying a word. He remains as kind and gentle a man as ever wore the uniform."

A Cooperstown-quality family man, too. Murphy and his wife, Nancy, have eight children—seven sons and Mallory, their youngest child and only daughter. The second oldest, Shawn, is a junior at Utah State and a starting offensive tackle for the football team. Murphy tries to watch Shawn play whenever possible, home or away—one weekend at San Jose State last season, the next at Louisiana Tech. "They're struggling," Murphy said of the Aggies. "They're trying to turn the program around."

Much like Murph and the Braves in the late '70s. And again in the mid-to-late '80s. Until that awful day in 1990, one Braves fans never

imagined would happen—the day Dale Murphy, the most decent and civil of all Braves, was traded. Shipped to that bastion of sports incivility, Philadelphia.

✳ ✳ ✳

"The first thing I think about are my early years—the early '70s—and coming up briefly in '76 and '77, then for good in '78," Murphy said. "The early days of Ted and Bobby."

That's Ted Turner, one of baseball's most unique owners, and Bobby Cox, the young manager Turner hired in 1979. "Everything was so new, and we were kind of struggling," Murphy said. "But Ted Turner always kept things kind of interesting."

Kind of? "He came into the clubhouse once and said, 'Murph, don't worry about that slump you're in. You're saving me a lot of money,'" Murphy said, laughing. "Right in front of everybody. You never knew what he might say.

"Ted was hilarious. Took care of us," Murphy continued. "I have no complaints about Ted. I know a lot of people wish he were back. People ask me a lot: 'What was it like to play for Ted?' He just wanted to win. Took care of players."

That was especially true for a fledgling catcher who was immensely talented—the 6-foot-5 Murphy could run, hit for power, and, seemingly, field his position—and whom Atlanta took with the fifth pick overall in the first round of the 1974 draft. "The next Johnny Bench." That's what some forecast for Murphy.

"The next position?" That's what the Braves wondered when Murphy began throwing the ball all around the field. Murphy developed a phobia: a fear of flying baseballs whenever he threw the ball back to the pitcher or to second base. Sometimes, the ball sailed into center field. Other times, pitchers ducked or hit the ground on the mound to avoid Murphy's attempt to nail a base stealer at second. When Murphy was still struggling with throws one day in spring training in 1978, his father, Chuck, said, "Don't worry, son, if they were trying to steal center field, you would've had them every time."

At 6-foot-5, Murphy may have been too big to be a catcher. Cox, the Braves' new manager, moved Murphy to first base, where he played most of that dismal '78 season. After struggling as a first baseman again in '79, with some catching on the side, Murphy—who tore a cartilage in his knee that season and missed a couple of months—found a new home. And Atlanta found a superb center fielder.

"He became a great outfielder," Cox recalled, "not a good one."

"I remember in the winter of 1979-80, Bobby called me up and said, 'Get ready to play the outfield,'" Murphy said. "Bobby giving me a shot in the outfield—that saved my career. He stuck with me, first moving to first base from catcher, then to the outfield.

"I remember Bill Lucas' patience, too," Murphy said of the Braves' late general manager. "I don't think I would've gotten a chance with another organization that would've stuck with me. It's hard in a game like this, competitive like it is and all that goes into it, that you have someone you really feel is in your corner and a friend.

"I was a scared kid from Portland, Oregon," he said. "I felt like Bill was really in my corner and pulling for me. He was great to me, hung in there and gave me a shot. It was a tough time for our organization, 'cause we were struggling. But Bill had a lot of faith in the young guys.

"Moving to the outfield, I was just grateful for the chance," Murphy said. "I felt I could contribute defensively. [The switch] helped me relax, gave me the opportunity to play and contribute."

Despite playing his third position in three years, Murphy opened the 1980 season optimistically. "I felt like I was coming into my own," he said. Indeed. Yes, Murphy again led the National League in strikeouts (133), as he had in 1978 (145). But he also hit 33 homers, the majority to right and right-center field. Plus he made the NL All-Star team for the first time, and Atlanta actually finished with a winning record (81-80) .

"But we had a strike in '81," Murphy recalled. "It was kind of a weird year. Going in, I thought, 'We're going to be okay.' But Bobby got fired, or whatever Ted [called it], and Joe Torre came in." At the press conference to announce Cox's firing, Ted Turner actually convinced Cox to attend his own managerial execution. Trying to describe what he was seeking in a new manager, Turner said, "If Bobby Cox weren't being fired, he'd be the best man for the job."

Instead it was Torre, who quickly became the beneficiary of what Cox was building. "This is Bobby Cox's team," Torre often told the press that season. Yet it was Torre's team that won its first 13 games, the best start in big-league history.

"We had had a little confidence building," Murphy said. "Even though it was a strike year in '81, we thought, 'Hey, we're building here.' In '82, we start out 13-0 and hey, we're pretty good."

Historically good. Hysterically, too. At least for one day in Cincinnati when little-used Rufino Linares, a quick, good-fielding outfielder, chased a drive in the left-center gap in extra innings of a tied ballgame. Linares dove and made a game-saving catch. Afterward, Linares happily recounted the play in his limited English: "I dive for ball. I look to left, no ball. I look to right, no ball. I look in glove, ball. I say, 'Rufi, you one lucky guy.'"

Murphy was fortunate, too, to play for Torre. Just as he'd prospered under Cox's tutelage, he continued to do so under Torre. "I started out well that year and Joe was great for me," Murphy said. "Joe and Bobby were two of the best to play for. I think I could've done well with Bobby, too. But I had my best year so far in '82."

In leading Atlanta back to the postseason for the first time in 13 years, Murphy tied for the NL lead in RBIs (109), was second in homers (36) and runs (113), third in total bases (303), fourth in walks (93), batted .281, and had 23 steals. He was the first Brave to play all 162 games in a season since Felix Millan in '69, won his first Gold Glove, and easily captured his first Most Valuable Player Award over runner-up Lonnie Smith. Murphy's lone disappointment was the NL Championship Series, where St. Louis swept Atlanta, 3-0.

The following season, the one downer was the Dodgers, who beat out Atlanta in the NL West by three games. Again, Murphy's numbers were phenomenal: a league-leading and career-best 121 RBIs, and a personal-high .302 average. He hit 36 home runs, led the league with a .540 slugging percentage, and was runner-up in homers (36), total bases, and runs. He played all 162 games again, won his second Gold Glove, and became the fourth man in National

League history—and the youngest—to join 30-30 clubs with 36 homers and 30 steals.

The Murph was unquestionably the best player in the National League in those two years and, arguably, for the decade of the '80s. "Winning two MVP's kinda surprised me," Murphy said. "Really. I was just coming from trying to figure out how to play the game, to switch positions and still be successful. As I look back on it, it kind of came out of the blue. I was struggling, trying to find my position.

"When I won the MVP in '82, I thought, 'Wow! This is crazy!'" he said. "But '83 was my better year. Obviously, it's the result of [playing for] good teams. With winning the MVP, at times there's a little controversy over who should win it."

Not those two years—especially in 1983, when Murphy easily out-polled runner-up Andre Dawson to repeat. "It was a big confidence booster," Murphy said. "But then you start feeling the pressure: 'Hey, what am I gonna do next year?' But I always thought, 'Just build on it. You can do it again.'"

The gushing had commenced during, and continued after, Murphy's first MVP campaign. Nolan Ryan said: "I can't imagine Joe DiMaggio was a better all-around player than Dale Murphy." Hank Aaron added: "Dale is probably the best all-around player in either league, probably the most valuable commodity in baseball right now." It continued after his '83 excellence, too. "He's the best I've ever seen, and I've seen Willie Mays," said Chicago Cubs pitching coach Billy Connors. "I've seen Murphy win games every way there is, a base hit in the ninth, a home run, a great catch, beating the throw to first on a double play. I've never seen anything like him before in my life."

When the 1984 season began, Murphy struggled, in part due to pressure to replicate his MVP seasons. "Yeah. You start to feel it," said Murphy, who was mired in an early slump. "You've got pressure on yourself, but you kind of block it out. But if you're not doing what you did last year, you're gonna hear about it."

That May, Murphy arrived later than usual to the ballpark one day, lugging his golf bag and clubs over his shoulder, then hustling to change and dress to take batting practice. A *Journal-Constitution* reporter, assigned to do the third story for the paper on Murphy's slow start, was waiting by his locker. That reporter—namely, me—explained his presence. Murphy politely excused himself, saying he had to get outside and take batting practice, but that he'd talk afterward.

"Okay, Murph," the reporter replied. "Sure," the reporter skeptically thought, then set off in search of others who'd assess Murphy's slump—including Luke Appling, the ancient Hall of Fame icon and Braves hitting consultant. When batting practice ended, Murphy returned to his locker and spied the reporter talking to Appling across the room. "Hey, Jack. Do you still want to talk?" Murphy asked. The reporter did. And talk they did, for nearly a half-hour.

"I just tried to keep hitting and playing, have a good attitude," Murphy recalls. "Take the good with the bad." Soon, the bad ended. For the third consecutive season, Murphy hit 36 home runs, tying Philadelphia's Mike Schmidt for the NL lead. He also led the league in slugging percentage (.547) and total bases. But, with the Braves finishing two games under .500, Murphy finished ninth in the MVP voting.

Then came 1985. Torre had been fired. The new manager was former Braves coach Eddie Haas. By mid-season, there was a popular bumper sticker around Atlanta: "No Mas Haas." For Braves fans, the last half of the '80s would be eerily, sickeningly reminiscent of the last half of the '70s.

"Yeah, it was tough, tough on everyone. No other way to put it," Murphy said of that season, which ended with Haas being fired, Bobby Wine cleaning up the managerial mess for the last month and a half of the year, and Atlanta freefalling to 66-96. "It was not a good time. We struggled in a lot of ways. We made some trades, guys got hurt. It kind of snowballed."

It was the first of six straight disastrous seasons for the Braves, in which they won more than 70 games just once, in 1986. Murphy, though, continued to shine—the lone beacon, as Stan Kasten would later recall, in the darkness. In 1985, he won the NL home run crown with 37. He led the league in runs scored and walks, posted his second .300 season and fourth straight Gold Glove, drove in 111 runs, and kept his consecutive games streak intact. That summer, Murphy drew more All-Star Game votes than any player in either league.

His numbers dipped slightly in '86: 29 homers, 83 RBIs, a .265 average. Yet he kept the consecutive games streak alive. That April 29th, Murphy cut his hand on a seam in the outfield fence after making a catch. He needed nine stitches and seemed likely to miss a week or more. The following evening, however, Murphy hit a pinch-hit homer off the Mets' Doc Gooden; for one of the few times that season, the Atlanta-Fulton County Stadium crowd stood and roared. Back in the lineup the next day, Murphy played every game until he finally took a day off on July 9. From September 27, 1981 'til then, he'd played in 740 consecutive games.

By season's end, the Braves were desperate, and would be for four more seasons. No help was coming, however—at least not from outside the organization. "Collusion really hurt us," Murphy said. "We really needed some help. I don't remember the exact years, but to try and get out of the rut we were in, we needed some [free agent] help. For a couple of years there, we couldn't get any."

Murphy doesn't hold the Braves accountable for a league-wide conspiracy. "I fault the commissioner, [Peter] Ueberroth," said Murphy. "The courts eventually ruled in [the players'] favor. But it was tough on [the Braves], and then it prolonged our slump.

"It was a frustrating time," he said. "We started struggling, and it snowballed. I don't believe the whole thing was [caused by] collusion. We started our slump before collusion, but it helped prolong it."

In 1987, under new manager Chuck Tanner, Murphy was named the team captain, switched from center field to right field, and continued to excel, hitting a career-high 44 homers, with 115 walks, and a .295 average. All of his offensive statistics ranked near the top in the NL. That same season, Andre Dawson, the All-Star outfielder desperate to escape Montreal, had signed a blank, or fill-in-the-salary, contract with the Cubs. He responded with an MVP season, and a long-term contract. All Murphy could do was wonder what might have been.

"There were a couple of years when Andrew Dawson and Tim Raines [Dawson's Expos teammate and fellow All-Star], the talk was they wanted to come to Atlanta," he said. "Why didn't they talk to them? We needed the help. But as I said, I don't blame the Braves. I blame Ueberroth."

In 1988, Murphy's power numbers dipped significantly (24 homers, 77 RBIs, .421 slugging percentage), just as his average plunged to .226. Following arthroscopic surgery in the off-season, Murphy moved back to center field in '89, collected 20 homers and 84 RBIs for a team that won just 54 games, but batted only .228. Still, he hit two three-run home runs in the sixth inning against San Francisco that July 27, tying the then-league record for RBIs in an inning. He became the first Brave to hit two homers in an inning since Bobby Lowe in 1894. Murphy was one of just three players [joining Eddie Murray and Darrell Evans] to hit 20 homers or more nine times in the '80s. For the decade, he was second in homers (308) and RBIs (929), fifth in hits (1,553), and played in all but 20 of the Braves' 1,557 games.

For Murphy, the '90s in Atlanta would be brief. "It was really hard. I was struggling. I went to Bobby Cox [who'd come down from his general manager's office midway through the season to replace Russ Nixon as the manager]," Murphy said. "I felt I needed to move on. It's difficult when a guy's struggling late in his career.

"I made it easy on them," he said. "I said, 'Bobby, I'm going. I'm going next year as a free agent. If you can get something for me, that's great.'"

On August 4, Murphy, 34, was traded to Philadelphia, along with pitcher Tommy Greene. In return, the Braves received pitcher Jeff Parrett and players-to-be-named-later, Jim Vatcher and Victor Rosario. The best Brave of the '80s, and arguably the game's player of the decade, was gone.

"It was hard to leave, but I needed to move on," said Murphy, who, on the night of his trade, tearfully addressed his teammates, many of whom had tears in their eyes themselves. "It kind of rejuvenated me. It was good to play somewhere new."

In '91, Murphy played 153 games, hit 18 homers, drove in 81 runs, and batted .252. But that was also the season when the Braves miraculously went from worst-to-first and nearly won the World

Series. And Murphy was in Philly, on the outside looking in. Yet in essence, after all the losing, he never wondered, "Why not me?" Rather, "Good for them."

Knee surgery in 1992 limited Murphy to 18 games that season. His two homers that year left him with 398. He would never hit another. Still struggling to regain his form after knee problems, unsure of a roster spot, Murphy made it easy for the Phillies, too, who released him. The same day—April 3, 1993—Murphy signed with the expansion Colorado Rockies. Murphy's recollection? "Yeah, I'll give it a whirl."

"I was pinch hitting," he said. "That's bad. After a while, they said, 'This isn't working out.'"

Even in Denver's rarefied air, Murphy's power was virtually gone. He played but 26 games, batted just .143, and retired in late May. He was 37, with 398 home runs, two shy of 400 and then 27th on baseball's all-time homer list. Murphy, who wept the morning he made his decision, cited "hundreds of hanging sliders I should have hit." He recalled, "If you can't hit one out of Mile High Stadium as a right-hander, you can't hit one out anywhere. My knee wasn't feeling well, so I hung it up.

"I felt, 'I can't go through all this just to hit a milestone, a benchmark number,'" Murphy said. "Number one, it was 400. That's not as much of a milestone. If I had been [close to] 500, I might've kept playing. Of course, if I'd had 498, I'd be happy with that.

"Number two, being away from my family was tough," he said. "Nancy was expecting our eighth child, our daughter. We were living south of Atlanta."

Like many athletes, though, retirement was an adjustment. "It wasn't as easy as I thought it was gonna be," Murphy said. "I was looking forward to what was going to be next in my life. That first year, I felt kind of lost. I thought, 'Maybe I could still play. DH.' It wasn't as easy as I thought—to be done at 37, with what I knew and did best.

"It was great just to have my time, and to be able to do certain things," he said. "Watch the kids play, and coach 'em. But then you realize you're never going to get it out of your blood. Now, I'm 50. I get around the ballpark and the boys, and I still miss it. . . . But not to the extent it dominates my life. I'll never get it out of my blood."

For three years at the end of the decade, Murphy was literally on a mission from God: a three-year mission in Boston for the Mormon Church, in charge of 600 missionaries working in New England. "That was a great experience for us, to be around the young men and women with the missionary. A faith-building experience," Murphy said. "Living in New England, too." The entire family moved there at first in the summer of 1997; then the two oldest boys went home to Utah to finish high school.

"We lived in Belmont, about 15 minutes outside Boston," Murphy said. "We loved living there. Boston's an incredible place, really has a super feel to it. It would've been a great place to play."

Especially with the Green Monster, the short, inviting left field wall in Fenway Park. "How did it look? It looks pretty close," Murphy said, laughing. "That would've been nice. I hit so many balls to right field, though, I don't know if I'd have been able to take advantage of it."

These days, Murphy makes appearances nationwide, many at baseball-related events. He does public speaking, too. "I like speaking to companies," said Murphy, who also has "a couple of small business things" on the side. He and Nancy find Utah the ideal place to raise their children.

Murphy has also considered entering politics. He's been approached a few times, first to run for the House of Representatives, later to run for governor. "I thought about it pretty seriously, for six, eight months," he said. "I talked to a lot of people. Then I thought, 'It's not really in me.' People said, 'If it's not in you, then forget about it.' Now, maybe someday, when the kids are grown. . . .'"

Although Murphy, a Republican, lives in "the most Republican county in the most Republican state in the country," his incumbent Congressman is a Democrat. "The guy's really tough to beat," Murphy said, chuckling. Being governor of Utah might be an even more daunting task, but at least he'd get to live at home, near the state capital in Salt Lake City.

Congress would be another matter. "If you win in Congress, you're never home," Murphy said. "And being governor, I just never felt prepared for that. I wouldn't rule it out, but I'm not planning on it."

Instead, he'll simply be Murph: One of five Braves whose number (3) is retired, the greatest Brave not enshrined in Cooperstown, and as good a man as ever wore the uniform. As Joe Torre once said, "Dale Murphy is the closest thing to the All-American boy."

GAME OF MY LIFE

"There's a couple of games that come to mind. I hit a home run late in the season against the Dodgers in '82, against Rick Honeycutt. It was on the road, in L.A., and we really needed a victory. That gave us a split in that series. I also hit two three-run homers in an inning against the Giants in '89, when I was really struggling. Man, that was crazy.

"But as far as the game of my life, I'd have to narrow it down to the day I stole my 30th base. I went 30-30. It was against the Dodgers [on September 24, 1983, at Atlanta-Fulton County Stadium]. I don't know who was pitching."

Bob Welch started the game and retired Murphy three times. But in the bottom of the ninth with the score tied 2-2, Tom Niedenfuer was on the mound for L.A. when Murphy coaxed a one-out walk, then stole second.

"I'd stolen 23 bases the year before," Murphy recalled. "Back then, 30-30 was pretty unique.

"When I was on first, I don't really remember thinking more than, 'I've got to try this.' I took off and stole my 30th."

With first base open and Murphy now on second, the Dodgers elected to intentionally walk Chris Chambliss. That brought up shortstop Rafael Ramirez, a .297 hitter that season, who promptly singled to left to drive in Murphy, the game-winning run.

"It was a satisfying thing," Murphy recalled of his 30th stolen base. "We had struggled so much that season, and I tried to help the team.

I took pride in my base running, stealing bases. And that was another way to help your team.

"As for my consecutive games streak, that was fun to be a part of, too. That created itself. I didn't plan on that," Murphy said, chuckling.

Just as the Atlanta Braves never planned on a can't-throw catcher turning out to be a franchise center fielder. The very best of Braves in the worst of times, Murphy belongs in Cooperstown.

ACKNOWLEDGMENTS

Somewhere, Fitz and Jack are smiling. My late, great parents instilled in me a love for baseball—and the Brooklyn Dodgers—shortly after I left the womb. The ticket stub, framed, hangs on our den wall: a $3 lower box seat in Ebbets Field, dated Tuesday, June 7, 1955—the day before my fifth birthday and the date of my first big-league baseball game. My father certified the ticket in handwritten blue ink: "Jack Jr."

Thanks to my sister, the beautiful Kathleen, for all of my games she came to and watched, and who let us monopolize the TV ("Lets Go Mets!") at home. And to our baby brother, Tom, the fierce competitor and superb athlete, once my constant shadow and later one helluva landlord who helped me get through the dark days.

To the good folks at Sports Publishing, especially John Humenik, who's been there and understood; Doug Hoepker, a terrific editor and good guy, even for a Cardinals fan; and Lance Birch, marketing's next Bill Veeck.

Nobody has a broadcast booth like the Braves. Nobody. Not with Skip, Pete, Joe, and Chip. And, for years, Uncle Ernie. And here's to baseball's next great play-by-play voice: Listen up, Seattle, to Dave Sims.

In memory of Marshall Mann, Jack Lang, and Van McKenzie.

What better way to spend a summer's day then sitting in the Turner Field press box, for a midweek matinee alongside The Bish, Stinny, Hummer, Schultzie (Jeff or Jim), Carroll, and even Bill ("That's AWFUL!") Zack, who went out of his way, and above and beyond, to help the new guy on the Braves beat.

There's no place like home games on the Party Row, beside Patty, J.D., and Easy Edgar, with periodic cameos by Moose.

Thanks to Bill Acree and his son Ben, John Holland and Fred Stone, Bubba and Dave Pursley, Chris Van Zant, and Dr. Joe. To the Serras, Carolyn and Glen. To the Walters, Banks and Victor. We all miss Anne McAlister, who was wronged but rose above it, and Carolyn King's sweet music on the organ.

To other denizens of other press boxes, especially Marty Noble, Ira Berkow, Paul Hagen, Marty Appel, Tracy Ringolsby, and, of course, The Commish—Rick Hummel, the only guy from St. Louis who'll be inducted into the Baseball Hall of Fame this summer.

Remember the true believers: Gary Caruso and everyone at *Chop Talk*; and the Braves 400 Club, the original Atlanta fans who keep Sid & Frankie Day alive every October 14th.

To the Atlanta baseball seamheads: Angelo Fuster, Jonathan Shils, Gen. Larry Taylor, Mark Slockett. Lynn and Candace Fowler, Paul Hemphill and Susan Percy. C.J. and Barbara, Doc and Dot. And the Bills, Rankin and Torpy, and Colleen McMillar, who all made the transition bearable.

Thanks to Bobby Cox and his coaches, and John Schuerholz.

To the standup guys, win or lose: Glavine, Maddux, Grissom, Smoltz, Justice, Blauser, Pendleton, Olson, the Lemmer, Chris Reitsma, and especially Mark Wohlers.

To the 20 men in this book who all talked so openly. My thanks.

And, most of all, to Janet, for saving me and restoring my love of the game; and to our daughters, Katharine and Ali, and the sweet memories of '91 and beyond, and those yet to come. Thank God for recessive sportswriter genes.

PHOTO CREDITS

DAVID JUSTICE: *OTTO GREULE JR./GETTY IMAGES*

BOB HORNER: *RONALD C. MODRA/SPORTS IMAGERY/GETTY IMAGES*

MARK LEMKE: *AP IMAGES*

ALBERT HALL: *AP IMAGES*

PHIL NIEKRO: *DIAMOND IMAGES/GETTY IMAGES*

STEVE BEDROSIAN: *RICH PILLING/MLB PHOTOS VIA GETTY IMAGES*

LEO MAZZONE: *MARK GOLDMAN/ICON SMI*

RON GANT: *BERNSTEIN ASSOCIATES/GETTY IMAGES*

GREG OLSON: *FOCUS ON SPORT/GETTY IMAGES*

PETE VAN WIEREN: *ATLANTA BRAVES*

SKIP CARAY: *ATLANTA BRAVES/MLB PHOTOS VIA GETTY IMAGES*

LONNIE SMITH: *AP IMAGES*

HENRY AARON: *AP IMAGES*

GENE GARBER: *AP IMAGES*

RALPH GARR: *AP IMAGES*

TERRY PENDLETON: *AP IMAGES*

TOM GLAVINE: *AP IMAGES*

CHARLIE LEIBRANDT: *KEN LEVINE/GETTY IMAGES*

JEFF BLAUSER: *AP IMAGES*

DALE MURPHY: *SCOTT CUNNINGHAM/GETTY IMAGES*

Celebrate the Heroes of Baseball & Georgia Sports in These Other Releases from Sports Publishing!

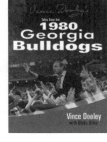
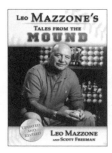